Rebecca Gausnell

Rebecca Gausnell is a freelance voice and dialect coach. She has worked in theatre, film and television in the UK, USA, France, Germany, Spain, the Czech Republic, Hungary, Croatia and Serbia.

Rebecca was born and raised in the United States and studied acting at Northwestern University in Chicago before completing her MFA in Voice Studies at the Royal Central School of Speech and Drama in London. She is a specialist in North American accents and works with actors to integrate good acting with good dialect work, which is both a technical and emotional process.

As a voice and dialect coach, Rebecca has worked with actors including Richard Armitage, Zawe Ashton, Orlando Bloom, Jerome Flynn, Johnny Flynn, Caroline Goodall, Kit Harington, Rhys Ifans, Thomas Kretschmann, Jack McBrayer, Mikael Persbrandt, Noomi Rapace, Clive Rowe, Noah Schnapp, Ed Skrein and Lydia Wilson.

She has worked with directors across all mediums including Gemma Bodinetz, Stephen Daldry, Matthew Dunster, Simon Evans, Yaël Farber, Neil Jordan, Diane Paulus, Lindsay Posner, Guy Ritchie, Michael Roskam, Melly Still and Mike Tweddle.

THE COMPACT GUIDES

are pocket-sized introductions for actors and theatremakers, each tackling a key topic in a clear and comprehensive way. Written by industry professionals with extensive hands-on experience of their subject, they provide you with maximum information in minimum time.

Published – or upcoming – titles include:

BREAKING DOWN YOUR SCRIPT
Laura Wayth

GETTING INTO DRAMA SCHOOL
Nick Moseley

GETTING, KEEPING & WORKING WITH YOUR ACTING AGENT
JBR

IMPROVING & MAINTAINING YOUR EMOTIONAL HEALTH
Andy Barker, Brian Cooley & Beth Wood

LEARNING YOUR LINES
Mark Channon

MAKING SOLO SHOWS
Lisa Carroll & Milly Thomas

MASTERING AN AMERICAN ACCENT
Rebecca Gausnell

The publisher welcomes suggestions for future titles in the series.

MASTERING AN AMERICAN ACCENT:
THE COMPACT GUIDE

Rebecca Gausnell

NICK HERN BOOKS
London
www.nickhernbooks.co.uk

A Nick Hern Book

Mastering an American Accent: The Compact Guide
first published in Great Britain in 2022
by Nick Hern Books Limited, The Glasshouse,
49a Goldhawk Road, London W12 8QP

Copyright © 2022 Rebecca Gausnell

Rebecca Gausnell has asserted her moral right
to be identified as the author of this work

Designed and typeset by Nick Hern Books, London
Printed and bound in the UK by
Mimeo Ltd, Huntingdon, Cambridgeshire PE29 6XX

A CIP catalogue record for this book
is available from the British Library

ISBN 978 1 84842 978 9

Dedicated with love to my two boys

Contents

Introduction	9
1. The Mouth	21
2. The Sounds	49
Consonants	
The Consonant R	51
The Consonant L	77
The Consonant T	85
Vowels	
TR<u>A</u>P and B<u>A</u>TH	95
SP<u>A</u>, L<u>O</u>T and TH<u>OU</u>GHT	101
G<u>O</u>AT	107
The Details	111
3. The Music	123
4. The Performance	143
5. Accent Warm-up	161
Full List of Practice Sentences	167
The Kit List	175
International Phonetic Alphabet Chart	177
References	180
Referenced Plays	181
Acknowledgements	182

Illustrations

Marie-Charlotte Brédon Nightingale

Recordings

Ace Anderson

Adriano Cabral

Hanna Gaffney

Eric Jerome Harper

Anne Hollister

Deirdre McLaughlin

Michael Silberblatt

Joel Trill

Will Wilhelm

Introduction

This book is for actors looking to learn a General American accent for performance. And whilst the text is aimed towards native speakers of English, multilingual actors may also find greater understanding of American English through the exercises.

Accent work is notoriously difficult, and many actors feel daunted by the task. It is not always obvious how to learn an accent. Some people are good mimics, but most require structured practice to hone the skill. And yet, during this work, actors can run into opposing objectives. The muscles of the mouth must move precisely, but without undue effort. The rhythms and melodies of an accent must be attended to, but not to an extent that overpowers the words being spoken. The accent is drilled tirelessly so that it may eventually be invisible in performance. Ultimately, the actor aims to embody an accent in every way – weaving pronunciation, muscular action, vocal musicality and an awareness of culture seamlessly into character and performance.

This book functions as an introduction to a General American accent. By detailing my approach to accent work, I hope to dispel misconceptions around learning a new accent. You *can* learn a new accent – and the process can be fun.

What is 'General American'?

In the entertainment industry and linguistically speaking, 'General American' is the term used to describe a group of vowels, consonants, grammar and vocabulary typical of many people from the United States. General American is often abbreviated to 'GenAm'. General American is a purposefully vague term because the accent is considered to be non-regional. Bizarrely, this means that General American is an American accent from nowhere. This is different to other accents in the United States that tend to be classified based on region or by the ethnic group from which the accent originates.

Because of its non-regional features, General American is often considered a standard accent in the United States. In fact, the accent is sometimes called General American or Standard American interchangeably. That is not to say that the accent is neutral or more valid than other American accents. However, the accent does carry a level of prestige in the United States. A General American accent is typical of most-likely educated, often white, usually middle- to upper-middle-class Americans from around the country. But that doesn't mean that all General American accent speakers fit neatly into those boxes.

The key here is the regional ambiguity of the accent. The accent expresses that the speaker is American without saying where they are from in the United States. A person could be from California or Vermont yet still speak with the universal features of the accent. In fact, the accent has been referred to as a 'newscaster' accent because TV anchors, regardless of the state, often speak with the accent. The accent also dominates American film and television today and is often called upon for American auditions.

You might notice as you listen to the accent that there is a range of voices that fall into the 'General American' category. Indeed, the accent is more of a continuum of accents, not a single unified sound. It is an umbrella term that encompass the most widespread American accent.

All of the following speakers have a General American accent but may sound slightly different from one another. This is because a person's voice is influenced by many factors, including age, gender and lived experience. Listen to this recording of General American voices speaking the same text to hear this in action.

▶ 1.1: *The Wonderful Wizard of Oz*

Because of the varying sounds, American dialect expert Dudley Knight called the dialect 'So-Called General American'. Knight's tongue-in-cheek nickname highlights the malleability of GenAm. Despite this fact, the dialect remains an industry standard catch-all to define a certain non-regional American sound.

This book coaches the general patterns that make up a General American accent. However, specificity is key. I encourage you to use recordings and audio from primary-source speakers to hone your practice. Keep in mind that the perfect American accent does not exist. Every speaker is different, and it is the actor's job to find an American sound that suits the character. Instead of searching for perfection, I would much prefer that the main features of the accent are present and that the accent sits comfortably in your mouth and voice.

Can You Really Learn an Accent from a Book?

After all, a book cannot speak! It may seem counter-intuitive to use a book as a teacher because an accent concerns the voice. It's true that a lot of accent training involves conscious mimicking and ear training. Think of this book like a road map for practising at home. Each chapter examines a specific feature of the accent and gives structured practical exercises. The book starts by establishing the foundations of a General American accent. It then transitions to applying the exercises to text. Finally, I address using the accent in performance.

In order to guide your learning, there is supplemental audio material and practical drills which you can access online so that you can listen to the target sounds and repeat for practice. Accents are inherently something you *hear*. The audio files provide a clearer and richer learning experience throughout.

Whenever the following symbol appears ▶ visit the following link online and play the relevant track number to hear the General American accent in action: bit.ly/mastering-an-american-accent-audio-recordings

Listen to these exercises, examples and extracts which will allow you to hear the sounds, consonants, vowels or music you need to make. Follow along; repeat after the speaker; keep practising...

How to Use This Book

As you begin, it is best to identify your goals and your time frame working with an accent. If you are beginning a practice regimen, I recommend you spend time on each chapter before moving to the next. Master one sound or concept at a time. The concepts build on one another, so having one mastered before moving on to the next will give you a sense of direction and progress. I advise starting at the beginning with Chapter 1: The Mouth before anything else. Accent work is physical, so having a connection with the muscles of the mouth will help ground yourself and your body in the accent. You can then work through the vowel and consonant rules with the associated drills and practice text. However, if you are already versed in the basics you may feel the urge to skip ahead. Chapter 3: The Music may be a good place to start for those who enjoy learning an accent by ear.

You may have an upcoming audition and need some quick ways into the accent. In that case, I suggest heading directly to some of the drills and practice sentences to consolidate the target sounds quickly. Then apply the exercises directly to your audition text.

It may be tempting to try to finish this book quickly, but I suggest against it. There are many moving parts to an accent, and the brain and mouth muscles can easily get tired. Accent work is best approached *little and often*. Ten minutes daily over the course of a week can be more effective than a single one-hour practice session. Do not discount the role of repetition in voice work. It is only through repetition that we achieve mastery.

Drills and Exercises

The guided drills and exercises throughout the book allow you to practise each new concept in isolation. These exercises will be signposted along the way. Gradually these concepts are expanded and applied to longer extracts from American plays.

There are many artists who may be opposed to the idea of drills. This is usually out of a fear that the drills will be done in a rote way and will lead to bad habits. However, you can avoid this by approaching the drills with attention and connection. Using drills wisely will free you from thinking about the accent in performance. Not unlike an athlete doing reps in a gym, drills build and prepare the muscles to work with ease. And just as the athlete completes their workout with alertness and precision, I encourage you to attend to the accent drills with the same level of aliveness. It is through conscious drilling that the muscles learn to respond.

I'm inviting you to think of a new accent as choreography for the mouth. By working on foundational movements, the dance becomes easier to the dancer. Speech is equally physical. What is different is that you speak every day, and these are muscles that you use and engage with ease already. You have reason to be confident when working with the muscles of speech through the technical sections. The biggest mistake I feel actors make in performing with an accent is a lack of technique to solidify the work. I promise that technique will only strengthen your ability to integrate the accent into your voice and your performance.

You can find recordings of these drills and texts online, with relevant recordings highlighted along the way. I suggest you periodically record yourself speaking alongside the recordings. Then go back and check your accuracy against the speaker. At times you may hear small errors that were not at all obvious to you whilst you were speaking. This is the opportunity for you to begin making changes.

Understanding an Accent

When working on an accent there are three distinct areas of practice:

1. The *mouth setting* of the accent. This can be understood as the shape and position taken by the muscles of speech when speaking in the accent.
2. The *sounds* of the accent, made up of *vowels* and *consonants*.
3. The *music* of the accent, which includes the rhythm, the stressing, the melody, pitch, volume, pace, vocal quality and the intonation patterns particular to an accent.

All three of these elements combine to form the technical side of learning an accent. Each can be actively trained and are the first steps to learning the accent in this book.

Areas of Practice

This book begins by looking at the *mouth*. An accent's mouth setting is the foundation of the entire accent, and a good place to return to if you hit roadblocks. The Mouth chapter is a fundamental first step in perfecting your American accent. I can assure you that if the accent's mouth shape is off, the desired accent will be difficult to achieve with ease. The mouth setting is comprised of the muscles of the mouth and face. It includes how the muscles shape the voice and sounds coming out of the mouth. The mouth's setting forms the basis of the entire accent, so I encourage you to give time and space to finding it in your own muscles.

The book then shifts to exploring the *consonants* and *vowels* or the *sounds* of the General American accent. These chapters guide you in a series of practical exercises in order to consolidate the main sounds in your own voice. Specific practice is explored through drills, tongue-twisters, and using extracts from some contemporary American plays.

The final technical section involves the *music* of a General American accent, where I lay out key concepts on the rhythm, stressing, melodies and intonation patterns of the accent. I also guide you through additional ways to develop your solo practice at home. Admittedly, the music of any accent can be difficult to practise as there are few definitive rules. However, our ears tend first to identify accents based on the overarching music of a voice. This is why mastering the music of an accent can go a long way in convincing your audience. It can also be vital to feeling confident when performing in the accent.

There is one final piece of the puzzle to any accent, which is the inherent *culture* of the accent. This includes consideration of the people who speak with the accent, along with the accent's geographical and historical background. We always hope that this element is already embedded in the character through compelling and accurate writing on the part of the playwright. However, it is the actor's job to bring that character to life in a truthful manner. At the end of the book I talk more about integrating an accent into your performance. Keep in mind that in order to sound fully American you will also need to embody an American character in performance. An accent is more expansive than the sum of its parts. The lived experience of a character should always be considered when developing your performance.

The Art of Learning an Accent

As you work your way through this book, I encourage you to approach the accent in four ways:

1. Conscious Listening
2. Conscious Feeling
3. Conscious Voicing
4. Conscious Visualising

The act of *Conscious Listening* comes into play because *you cannot reproduce a sound you cannot hear*. It is only through listening that you can begin to approach an accent and understand it fully. Often the accents to which we have been most exposed prove the easiest to recreate. Even your own natural accent developed due to listening to your environment, your parents and your peers. Conscious Listening gives you exposure to the target sounds and music of the accent in order to reach this level of mastery.

Accent work concerns the muscles of speech, so *Conscious Feeling* develops awareness around these muscles so they can move with ease and precision in the accent. Take notes as you go on how the target sounds *feel* in your mouth. You may even want to assign a shape or picture to that feeling so that you can recreate the sound in the future. You could also find it useful to use a small personal mirror or a smartphone camera on selfie mode to see the mouth at work when making a new sound. Having those shapes in the mind's eye will help develop and clarify an accent so that you can hit the target sound every time.

Conscious Voicing might also be described as mimicking or copying the sounds aloud with heightened awareness. Speaking in the accent aloud is important in order to begin rooting the accent in your own voice and body. A big mistake actors can make is practising the accent in silence. Although it may seem safer to stay quiet, you will master an accent by taking it on the road. Practise out loud in order to make strides towards a fully realised accent.

Conscious Visualising allows you to see and feel the accent at work in your own body. It may also give you the space to create your own images to aid the Listening, Feeling and Voicing work. Conscious Visualising will be different for everyone, but it can be an imaginative process that connects the accent to the body, breath, and voice. Perhaps you consider the elements of character – such as movement, pacing or breath – and begin marrying these with accent work. The ways into Conscious Visualising are infinite, and will be looked at more in-depth in Chapter 4: The Performance.

To be clear, you are not responsible for thinking about all of these points all of the time while practising an accent. There may be certain ways of working that you favour, and the preferred way will be different for everyone. Having an idea of your own learning styles can go a long way when undertaking a new skill. I suggest you experiment with all four approaches in order to create a well-rounded way in to learning an accent.

Thoughts on Phonetics

English is not written phonetically. This means that the words are not pronounced in the exact way they are written. The good news is that the English language has a range of accepted pronunciations, meaning lots of different accents occur within the language. But this range of choices can become tricky when approaching accent work. Just because a word is written a certain way does not mean you can count on the letters to guide you on the pronunciation.

For example, all of the following words are written with the letter A, but the letter A can be pronounced differently in each word:

have, palm, paper

And in this sentence, two words are spelt 'close' but pronounced differently:

Close the door that is *close*.

To overcome this problem, an entirely new alphabet was created called the International Phonetic Alphabet (often abbreviated to IPA). The phonetic alphabet is useful because it employs one phonetic symbol to notate a singular sound. This concept may make sense to musicians who are used to notating sound. However, exclusive use of the phonetic alphabet can lead to frustration for some. For one, it can be time-consuming to learn an entirely new alphabet. Moreover, the phonetic symbols can look very similar to each other which can be discouraging to people with dyslexia or differing learning styles.

A British linguist named J.C. Wells created a system called the Kit List which simplifies the process of notating the vowels of English. The Kit List is a basic list of words, with each word representing a vowel sound in the English language with Received Pronunciation as its reference. The Kit List is not fixed like the phonetic alphabet, so the target sound may change depending on the desired accent. This means that some of the words represent the same sound in one accent, but different sounds in another. However, the list is useful because it gives consistent example words to represent vowels. In this book the Kit List words are used to represent the target vowel, and as a basis for the drills you will find throughout the text.

You can find the entire Kit List, along with a guide to the International Phonetic Alphabet, at the back of this book.

How Best to Notate Sound?

In this book I use three notation options:

1. 'Faux-netics': notation using the letters of the alphabet to write out a sound
2. Phonetics: the International Phonetic Alphabet
3. The Kit List: a word representing the target sound

These three options will always appear together so you can choose the option that you understand and that enhances your learning. Each sound is also recorded and you are encouraged to listen to the recordings for reference. You are also welcome to create your own way of notating the accent that makes sense to you. It is very common for actors to use a blend of these notation options, so feel free to mix them up as long as it makes sense to you.

Finally... Before Beginning

Embrace a sense of play and discovery in the work ahead. Children mimic voices all the time and have no hang-ups about getting them right or wrong. I encourage you to take on this same mindset when practising. Through play comes ease and freedom – freedom from self-doubt, from judgement and from self-critique.

A native speaker of an accent has found ease in their speech through years of practice. You are beginning your journey, and the best place to begin is at the beginning. Do not worry if a concept doesn't click on your first try. Try a new approach or return to the exercise later with fresh eyes. Meet the work with openness, and confidence will follow.

1. The Mouth

An essential part of accent work is to understand and gain mastery over the muscles responsible for sound and speech. Because the muscles of speech shape the sounds coming out of your mouth, even a small change to these muscles can lead to a big change in the sound of your voice and accent. These muscles are, in a sense, the physical 'tools' of accent work. Your 'tools' include your lips, tongue, soft palate, jaw and the muscles of the face. These muscles, alongside your voice, form an accent.

Up until now, you have used your muscles of speech for one particular way of speaking – speaking like you! Your muscles are experts in forming your unique voice and speech. The muscles most likely work without you having to think too much, and it probably feels easy to speak the way you do.

As you begin accent work, you are asking the muscles to work in a completely new way. Sometimes this can feel liberating, but at times our ingrained muscular patterns can hold us back from true fluency in an accent. Begin by releasing and engaging the muscles of speech so that they become flexible and adept in their movements for this American accent.

Five Areas of the Mouth

This chapter focuses on the following five areas:

1. The muscles of the face
2. The lips
3. The tongue
4. The soft palate
5. The jaw

I have separated out the five areas of the mouth for ease of approach. However, keep in mind that all five of these muscle groups connect with one another, meaning that the muscles of speech physically intersect with adjoining muscles. The exercises in this chapter develop awareness and precision over one 'tool' area so that it will work with ease as part of the whole.

Using a Hand-held Mirror

I encourage you to use a small hand-held mirror or a smartphone camera on selfie mode so that you can look at your own mouth as you work. It's often easier to first *see* speech in action by looking at your own mouth. Some actors may prefer to *feel* the muscles working without an image, but developing an awareness of both physical sensation and seeing the muscles in action can lead to quicker mastery of an accent.

Approaching the Exercises

An important part of this work is what British voice coach Barbara Houseman terms 'layering', where you focus on one element at a time in the exercise. After completing the exercise, you should let go of the element you have just explored, trusting that your body will retain the experience and the muscle memory of what you've learnt. You then move on to adding another layer and repeating the process. Use layering throughout this chapter by taking the exercises one at a time and trusting that your body will access what it needs to through the technique.

The mouth position of any accent is not fixed and rigid. These exercises are here to help you develop an overall American mouth shape. This mouth shape will help you more easily form the sounds of the accent. It may take a few rounds of an exercise before you feel you can let it go and move on to the next layer. That is perfectly normal, as muscle memory takes time to develop. Learning an accent is like going to the gym for your mouth; if you put in the training, the muscles respond.

With that being said, perfection is not necessary before moving on to the next exercise. Layering accent work is not about getting everything right on the first try, it's about strengthening the muscles and moving up through stages of ability. With consistent practice, the exercises will begin to get easier.

Warming Up

The following section is a warm-up before moving on to specific exercises for the General American accent. A warm-up is very important for preparing the muscles for the subsequent exercises; not only will it prime the muscles for practice, but the exercises also release muscular memory patterns before beginning. As tempting as it can be to skip a warm-up, spending time in this section will pay off in the long run.

When switching accents we want the muscles to move with ease. There are forty-three individual muscles that make up the structure of your face. Despite this high number of muscles, many people may be surprised to learn that they hardly ever change from their habitual way of speaking. Yet when performing in an accent the muscles must adjust – and if these muscles seem stuck or overly tense, the audience will start to doubt the fluency of your accent. Warming up leads to freedom and flexibility to shift the way you hold your mouth to speak with a new accent.

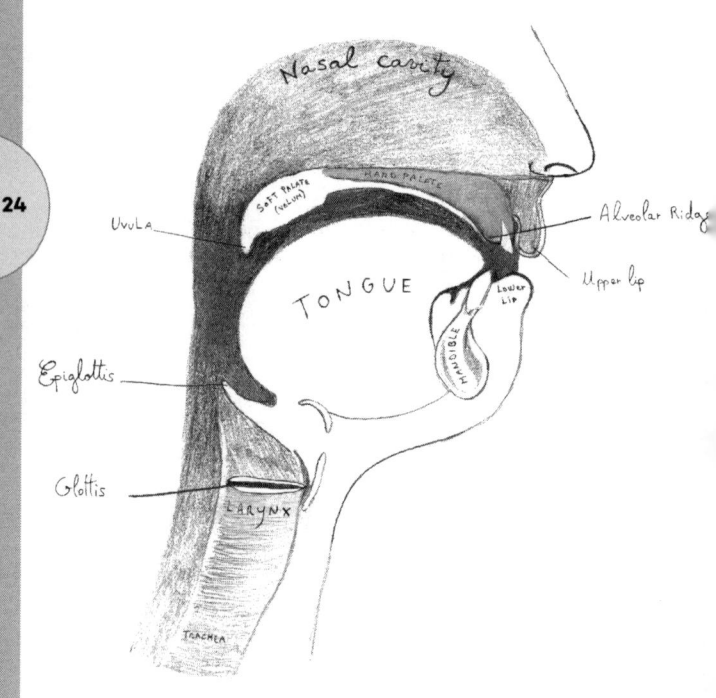

Warm-up: The Muscles of the Face

Face Warm-up

1. Initiate a gentle chewing motion with the jaw swinging free and your lips closed.
2. As you do this, raise and lower your eyebrows to engage the muscles of your forehead and around your eyes.
3. Then transition the movement into the area around your cheeks, tensing and releasing the muscle and tissues in your cheeks as if you are giving a big smile and then letting the smile fall.
4. Bounce between moving the eyebrows and moving the cheeks. See if you can do this whilst gently chewing with your jaw.
5. Check to be sure there's no excess tension in the back of your neck during this exercise. You can do this by keeping the shoulders released throughout the exercise. The only active muscular action should be in your face.

Tense and Release

1. As you continue to breathe, tense your entire face into a tight ball for a count of three seconds.
2. Release the tension, allowing the muscles of the face to return to where they want to be without 'placing' the muscles in any specific position.
3. Then spread the muscles of your face wide for a count of three seconds. Be sure to include your tongue in this stretch.
4. Release the tension, allowing the muscles of the face to return to where they want to be, again without 'placing' the muscles.

5. Repeat three times, taking care to be sure you are breathing throughout this exercise.

Warm-up: Full Face Massage

Temple Massage

1. Begin by gently massaging your temple area. This is located on either side of your head above your ears and just behind the eyes. You are massaging your temporalis muscles here. These muscles may seem very far from your mouth, but in fact the temporalis muscles connect with your jaw – and so the muscle plays a role in speech.
2. Allow for a sense of release and letting go in the jaw as you continue to massage the muscles on either side of your head.
3. Keep breathing as you massage this area for five to ten seconds.

Jaw Massage

1. Bring your hands down to massage your jaw. Locate the large muscle on either side of your face just in front of your ears. You are massaging your masseter muscles here. These are some of the strongest muscles in your body relative to their size. They are used to close the jaw for chewing food, after all!
2. Allow for a sense of release and letting go of any excess tension in the jaw as you continue to massage the area.
3. Keep breathing as you massage this area for five to ten seconds.

Sinus and Forehead Massage

1. Bring your hands forward to lightly massage your sinus area on either side of your nose. You might give some light taps with your fingertips to bring blood flow to the area.
3. Then transition your hands to massage your forehead. You can give light swipes up and out with your fingers to encourage a release of any tension being held in the forehead.

Lip Massage

1. Gently move your top lip back and forth with your hand in a massage motion in order to move and release the muscles in and around the top lip.
2. Then bring that action down to the bottom lip in order to give the same release to this area.
3. Gently trill your lips by blowing air through them in a 'Brrrr' action to release any excess tension. This action is sometimes described as 'horse lips'.

Warm-up: The Lips

Lip Isolations

1. Imagine you have a string attached to your top lip, and that this string is pulling the top lip up and away in isolation from the bottom lip. Release. Repeat three times.
2. Then transition to the bottom lip. As if you have a string attached to your bottom lip, imagine the string is pulling the bottom lip out away from your mouth. Release. Repeat three times.

3. As if you have a string attached to the right lip corner, imagine the string pulling the right lip corner out into a one-sided smirk. Release. Repeat three times. Then do the same isolation exercise on the left side.
4. I highly recommend using a mirror during this exercise to see the muscles in action.

Lip Movement

1. Open your mouth as wide as possible, feeling the sense of space between the lips.
2. Now move your lips into a rounded shape, as if they are forming a perfect circle. Move between spreading and rounding five times.
3. Push the lips forward into a pucker, as if you are kissing the air in front of you.
4. Then curl the lips in the opposite direction, as if you just licked a lemon, and are now pursing the lips in a compressed action.
5. Move between puckering and compressing the lips five times.
6. Continue to keep your breathing open and free throughout this exercise.

Warm-up: The Tongue

Tongue Stretch 1

1. Flatten the tongue completely with the sensation of releasing all tension from the front, middle and back of the tongue.
2. Slowly stretch the tongue forward and out of the mouth.

3. Count to ten aloud with the tongue resting gently on your bottom lip.
4. Then slowly ease the tongue back into the mouth whilst keeping the tongue completely flat. Sense a release in the body of the tongue.
5. Repeat three times, taking care to keep your breathing open and free throughout.

Tongue Stretch 2

1. Place the tip of the tongue behind the bottom teeth.
2. Ease the middle of the tongue forward and out of the mouth in order to feel a stretch in the back and the root of the tongue.
3. Ease the tongue back in the mouth and repeat this action three times.
4. Slowly add in some light sound from your voice to allow release in the back of the tongue when voicing during the stretch.
5. Take care not to engage your jaw during this exercise. The jaw should be comfortably released throughout, and you may want to place a hand on the jaw to encourage stillness. Allow the tongue to move in isolation from the rest of your mouth.

Tongue Shapes

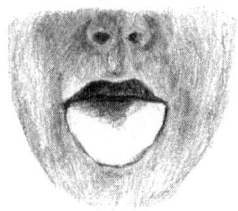 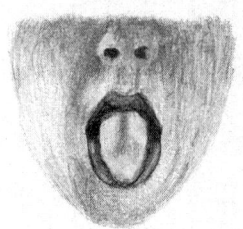

1. Flatten the tongue completely, as if you're making a pancake shape. Allow the tongue to hang out of the mouth.
2. Now point your tongue forward and out as if you are sticking it out at someone. Notice that the middle fibres of the tongue fatten up in this position and the tongue tip becomes pointed.
3. Move between these two shapes, flattening and bunching the tongue five times.
4. See if you can do this exercise completely isolated from the lips. That means the tongue is the only part of your mouth moving, without involving the lips in the process.

Tongue Circles

1. Place your tongue in the space between the top teeth and upper lip.
2. Then draw a circle with your tongue. It may feel like you are drawing your tongue around the numbers of a round clock inside your mouth. Draw between 12, 3, 6, and 9 o'clock to create a circular motion. Return back to 12 o'clock again on each rotation. You can imagine that you are cleaning your teeth with your tongue as you go.

3. Repeat four times to the right. Then reverse and repeat four times to the left.
4. Repeat two times to the right. Then reverse and repeat two times to the left.
5. Repeat once to the right. Then reverse and repeat once to the left.
6. Keep your neck long and released during this exercise and allow your breathing to be free and open. Maintain a softness in the jaw throughout.
7. You can swallow at the end of this exercise to release any residual tension. For some actors this exercise allows for a deep release in the tongue root.

Warm-up: The Soft Palate

Up until this point you probably have never needed to think about your soft palate, which is the squishy bit of the roof of your mouth as you head towards the back of the throat.

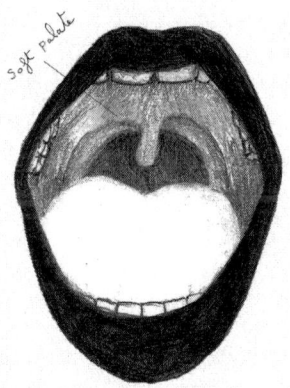

To find your soft palate: bring your tongue up directly to touch the roof of your mouth. You should hit a hard surface – that is your hard palate. Keep your tongue on the roof of your mouth, but begin to move the tongue back until you ease off of the hard surface and on to a softer one. That's your soft palate.

Soft Palate Yawn Stretch

1. Provoke a yawn (it can even be a fake 'actor yawn'!), but keep your lips together as you yawn. You should feel a stretch in the soft palate, which is located at the back of the mouth before the opening of the throat. It may feel as if it is expanding into a parachute shape.
2. Alternatively, you can encourage a yawn and keep your lips open if that seems easier. In that case, allow your tongue tip to rest behind the bottom teeth. This will lead to a greater stretch than if you yawned without the tongue resting down.

Soft Palate Exploration with the Voice

1. Imagine that you have some hot soup in your mouth and you are avoiding burning the roof of your mouth. Allow yourself to feel the soft palate rise.
2. With the soft palate raised in this position, you can add some gentle sound with your voice. You may be able to feel the sound vibrations in the mouth. If you speak with your soft palate up, your voice may sound 'denasal', as if you had a cold and your sinuses were blocked.
3. Then release that position and imagine your soft palate sinking down. It may feel like the soft palate is 'sagging' like a hammock in the back of your mouth.
4. With the soft palate lowered in this position, add some gentle sound with your voice with your mouth

open. You may be able to feel the sound coming up into the nose and vibrating the nose. Hear the nasality in your voice – you may sound like a goose honking!

5. Repeat the process a few times in order to encourage flexibility and mobility in the soft palate.

Warm-up: The Jaw

Jaw Release

In this warm-up I have combined two release exercises taught to me by British voice practitioners Annie Morrison and Barbara Houseman. The access point is to create an image or sensation for yourself that will encourage the jaw to let go of any tension or holding. Some examples might be:

- The jaw melting like hot butter.
- A sensation of getting into a hot bath at the end of a long day.
- A sensation of 'turning off' your brain to allow the jaw to release.

Hold on to your chosen image or sensation as you set up the exercise:

1. Place a clean wine cork between your front teeth. The wine cork should sit only slightly in your mouth so that you have enough space to move your tongue. If you don't have a wine cork, you may use one finger from your freshly washed hand.

2. Keep the chosen image or sensation in your mind's eye as you begin tongue isolations by forming sounds, all whilst lightly holding the cork between your teeth without biting down. This is training your tongue to move independently from your jaw.

3. Move the tip of the tongue: articulate a few Ts and Ds using the tip of the tongue as it makes contact with the gum ridge.
4. Move the middle of the tongue: articulate a YUH /j/ as in YES by gently lifting the blade of the tongue before releasing into the consonant.
5. Move the back of the tongue: articulate a few Ks and Gs using the back of the tongue making contact with the soft palate.
6. Stick with this exercise for two to three minutes – it may feel like a very long time! Continue to renew your connection with your image or sensation throughout the exercise. It should feel like the tongue is moving in isolation from all other areas of the mouth. You will notice your jaw is getting involved because you will be biting down on the cork or your finger.
7. When you finish the exercise, notice any changes felt or sensed in and around the jaw. Read a piece of text to bring those changes immediately onto spoken words.

The General American Accent Mouth

Here are some general rules regarding the mouth setting of a General American accent:

- The lips rest fairly flat, only rounding forward for a few specific vowels.
- The lip corners may feel as if they are slightly spreading, as if in a small smile.
- There is an overall sensation of widening and spreading in the mouth.
- The body of the tongue can move between a flat position to a bunched position.

- The tip of the tongue is broad, not too pointed or precise.
- The sides of the tongue can touch the inside of the upper molars.
- The tongue may hang in a bit of a hammock position between the upper molars.
- The soft palate can be flexible, raising and lowering as needed.

Allow yourself to visualise the mouth moving into these positions. It may help to close your eyes and allow the visualisation to move into each muscle so that your mouth takes on this new position. Begin to speak a few simple words and phrases in an American accent through this mouth setting:

One, two, three, four, five.

Monday, Tuesday, Wednesday, Thursday, Friday, Saturday, Sunday

Hey, how are you?

You may want to start speaking in a whisper to feel the shape of the oral posture before increasing the volume slowly.

Of course, the mouth is never fixed when we talk, but instead 'dances' around this position when speaking. Think of these descriptions functioning as the overall basis of the American mouth. It is the place where the accent returns to time and time again. This might even be thought of as the 'resting place' of the accent because these are the most familiar spots for the mouth in the accent.

Accent Exercises

Accent-specific mouth exercises are detailed here, as a guide to the American mouth position for each area explored in the warm-up.

Try all the exercises detailed below using the following monologue:

Avery from The Flick *by Annie Baker*

❝And the answer to every terrible situation always seems to be like, Be Yourself, but I have no idea what that fucking means. Who's Myself? Apparently there's some like amazing awesome person deep down inside of me or something? I have no idea who that guy is. I'm always faking it. And it looks to me like everyone else is faking it too. Everyone is always acting out some like stereotype of the person they're supposed to be. It's like we're all on a sitcom or something. All the time.

Accent Exercises: The Tongue

The tongue is an important part of the American accent because it directly affects the pronunciation of the consonant R and the consonant L. The middle and back of the tongue engage to create these consonants. It can feel like the action shifts to focus on the back of the tongue. (Refer to 'The Consonant R' and 'The Consonant L' sections for more information.)

The tongue in the American accent often sits high in the mouth, resting between the molars of the top row of teeth as if in a hammock position. It then moves into a bunched position for the consonants R and L.

As you practise, keep in mind that the tongue is not fixed and does not stay rigid in one spot in your mouth. The exercises are a way to guide your tongue into a position that may make the accent easier. After completing the exercise, notice if your tongue feels different. Observe any changes in your tongue as you re-read your practice text. Remember that you are building a muscle through these exercises.

Finding the American Tongue

1. Bring your tongue outside of your mouth so that the tongue rests on your bottom lip. Allow for a sense of release through the entire tongue.
2. Keeping your tongue flat on your bottom lip outside of your mouth, read the following sentence aloud.
3. Feel the middle and back of the tongue engaging in a bunch action to form the Ls and Rs. Keep the tip of the tongue resting down.

   Eleven yellow lemons rolled rapidly down the road.

4. Then place the tongue back in the mouth. Repeat the same sentence but keep the sense of action in the back of the tongue that you felt when you had the tongue out of the mouth.

You can also use this exercise when speaking the practice text in order to access the American tongue:

1. Keeping your tongue flat on your bottom lip outside of your mouth, read your practice text once through in the General American accent.
2. After you've read the text once through, go back to the top to practise the text sentence by sentence.

3. Read each sentence once with your tongue on your bottom lip and the tip of your tongue released.
4. Then place your tongue back in your mouth and keep the sense of action in the back of the tongue that you felt when you had it out of the mouth. Repeat the exercise on the next sentence. Continue this exercise back and forth through the whole text.
5. Finally, go back and read the entire text feeling a sense of ease in your tongue.

Some actors report feeling that the back of the tongue is overworking while speaking in an American accent. This could feel like a tension or a lump at the back of your throat near the tongue root. In this case, the above exercise can be used, but place your focus on releasing the back of the tongue. It will then release unwanted tension and to develop ease. After all, an accent that is not moving fluidly in the mouth will seem false to the listener.

High Tongue Position 1

You can train this high tongue position by exploring other consonants that lift the back of the tongue.

1. Start by voicing a few Ks, as in the word KICK: Kuh, kuh, kuh...
2. Then transition to a series of Gs, as in the word GO: Guh, guh, guh...
3. Next voice a series of -NGs, like at the end of the word SING: NG, NG, NG...
4. Finally, transition to the consonant R and sense the back of the tongue lift as it did in the previous steps. It may feel as if the tongue is trying to touch the soft palate: R, R, R...

High Tongue Position 2

1. Bring the sides of your tongue up to touch the inside edges of the top molars. It may feel as if your tongue is a hammock in your mouth, with the sides up and the middle forming a channel.
2. Start by speaking aloud on any topic in your own accent, keeping your tongue in place in this position.
3. Now transition to using the American accent. Read the practice text once through with your tongue in this position.
4. Finally, release the tongue but see if you can keep a sense of the exercise in your muscle memory. Read your practice text once through again. Note any changes that might have occurred.

Helpful Hint: Throughout this exercise, encourage release in your jaw. It may be useful to use a visual image or sensation to help achieve a sense of release, for example: imagining the jaw is melting like warm butter. Create your own visual image or sensation that makes most sense to you and your body.

Accent Exercises: The Lips

As a general rule, the lips of the American accent return again and again to a position that can be described as slightly spread from side to side, as if with the slightest hint of a smile. The centre of the lips may rest flat – neither overly puckering nor compressing. Of course, your lips will dance around this position when talking, but overall they will tend to sit wide and even a bit flat at times.

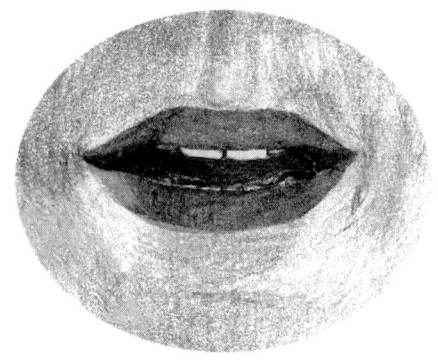

Remember that everyone has a different starting point based on their own way of speaking and the anatomy of their lips. Because the lips are very easy to see on a person, it is useful to watch the lips of an American speaker. Observe your lips when speaking in your own voice and note down the similarities and differences. Use that knowledge as an access point to shifting your mouth to meet the accent.

Lip Corner Spread

1. Imagine you have a string attached to each lip corner, gently pulling the corners out to the side.
2. Read the practice text all the way through, keeping a sense of the imaginary strings gently engaged.
3. Now release the imaginary strings but retain a small sense of what the feeling was like before. You can try this exercise a few times to find the appropriate amount of energy to put into the imaginary strings while speaking in the accent.

Sense of a Smile

1. As you transition from the Lip Corner Spread exercise with the strings, it may be also useful to feel a sense of a smile while speaking in the accent. This will raise the cheeks and encourage the lip corners to spread while speaking in the accent.
2. Focus on exploring the sense of a smile without too much tension. Some actors may experience undue tension at the lip corners. Be careful not to tuck the lip corners in as if fastening the lip corners down to the face, but rather allow for a sense of ease in this area.

Helpful Hint: Remember the sense of a smile is there to help your mouth find a landing position in the General American accent. It is not a fixed position.

Accent Exercises: The Soft Palate

The soft palate can raise and lower, which affects sound going into your nose. When sound waves escape through the open soft palate and into the back of the nose, the voice will sound nasal.

The soft palate is a muscle. You can move and control the soft palate, just as you do your arm or leg or even your tongue. It may not be the most precise muscle, but the soft palate can be developed for accent purposes.

Sense of Spreading

In the same way that you are training your lip corners and your tongue to spread side to side, so too can the soft palate be trained. Try this exercise to access that sensation in the back of your mouth:

1. Visualise a sense of spreading in the soft palate from side to side. It may feel as if the sides are lightly being stretched outwards, as if you were widening out a parachute.
2. Read a practice text once through with this sense of spread extending into the back of your mouth.

Nasality Practice

Although the General American accent should not be *overly* nasal, the accent does use nasality in one key place:

When the vowel /æ/ as in TRAP combines with the nasal consonants N, M, or NG, forming AN, AM and ANG. The American accent needs a soft palate that is flexible and free to move in order to make this sound.

Examples include:

AN	AM	ANG
can	ham	sang
man	damn	anger
Dan	Sam	tangle
candle	camera	rang
bandana	jam	language

1. Practise these words aloud. Allow yourself to feel the soft palate hanging low like a hammock.
2. You may even feel or visualise the sound travelling up and into your nose when speaking these words. Sense a buzz or vibration in this area.
3. From the front of your face allow yourself to feel the nasality through the vibration on the bridge of your

nose and along your cheekbones. Placing a hand on this area may help you physically feel the vibration as you speak the words aloud. I like to imagine the sound is popping out from my nose and cheekbones.

Accent Exercises: The Muscles of the Face

There isn't one set position for the muscles of the face in the General American accent, but you want the muscles of the face to move with ease when speaking. One way you can develop ease in an American accent is by first over-engaging the muscles of the face. By overaccentuating the action of the facial muscles, you will empower them to move with greater ease once you release that tension into speaking normally.

Pulling Faces

This exercise has also been called the 'Dory Speaking Whale in *Finding Nemo* Exercise' and the 'Treacle Mouth Exercise' by my students and clients.

1. Reading a piece of text aloud in an American accent, exaggerate the action of your mouth and facial muscles.
2. You can also extend out the vowel sounds as if moving very slowly through the words.
3. Check in to be sure this extra tension has not travelled to your neck. The overworking should stay in the face!
4. Finally, release your face and go back to read the entire text through as normal with a renewed sense of ease in your face muscles. Notice any changes that have arisen.

Helpful Hint: Many actors find it useful to try out a string of American swear words using this exercise! Swear words have a mix of consonants and vowels, plus we tend to exaggerate when using them. Moreover, the word choice can be unique from accent to accent. You might find that this approach helps to launch your mouth and voice into the accent.

Cork in the Mouth

In the following exercises, take care to hold the cork very lightly between your teeth. This exercise is about creating a sense of space and ease, not about biting into the cork.

1. Place a clean wine cork between your front teeth. The wine cork should sit only slightly in your mouth so that you have enough space to move your tongue. If you don't have a wine cork, you can use one finger from your freshly washed hand.
2. With the cork or finger in your mouth between your teeth, read the text aloud in the accent. Allow the muscles of the face to move as needed in order to make the words as clear as possible.
3. Encourage a sensation of release and spreading in the mouth.

Cork in the Mouth 2: Going Sentence by Sentence

After you've read the text once through, go back to the beginning, reading the text sentence by sentence.

1. Read a sentence once with the wine cork in the mouth.
2. Then remove the cork but keep the sense of space felt when you had the cork in the mouth.

3. Continue this back and forth through to the end of the text. This will help you get a feel for the space without the cork in your mouth.
4. Finally, go back and read the entire text without the cork in your mouth. Allow for a sense of ease in your face muscles and mouth.

Accent Exercises: The Jaw

Releasing the jaw leads to less muscle tension overall and more fluidity in the accent. While there are a few American sounds that require a closed jaw position, you don't want the accent to feel overworked by the jaw.

Helpful Hint: Everyone is starting from a different place based on their own voice and accent. For some actors, releasing the jaw in the General American accent may feel like a big change. For others, jaw release may not seem to make much difference. That is completely normal, and it could take some experimenting to settle on your personal sweet spot.

Jaw Release

1. Bring your hands up to touch either side of your face gently, resting on the jaw and cheeks.
2. Encourage a sense of letting go in your jaw. You can also use your hands to bring in the sensation of spreading from side to side explored in other parts of this chapter.
3. Read your practice text once in the accent while holding this position. It won't sound like the perfect accent – but that's okay! Focus on allowing your jaw to release and soften under your hands.

4. Release your hands from your face. Read the text again as normal, but retain a sense of the jaw release found above.

Troubleshooting

The tip of the tongue is doing all the work

The back of the tongue is highly active in the American accent, forming the distinctive consonants R and L. If the tip of the tongue is taking over, then the accent may feel like it's sitting too far forward in the mouth. Return back to the Finding the American Tongue exercise to reset the action of the tongue.

The lips are overly rounded

If your lips are overly rounded, the entire accent can sound a bit 'off'. This often happens if the speaker if using their lips as the main source of action with the accent being shaped at the front of their face. Place your index finger vertically on your lips and encourage the lips to release as you practise. Visualise shifting the action to the middle and back of the tongue, which should take some action out of the lips. Remember, the tongue is the leader here, not the lips. Return to the lip and tongue exercises to encourage a shift out of an overly rounded lip position.

The lip corners are tucked in

Some actors run into trouble when adopting the mouth position by adding excess tension in the lip corners. This may feel as if the lip corners are 'tucked in' or 'buttoned closed'. Release tension in the lip corners by blowing the lips out a few times like horse lips on a Brrrr lip trill, taking care to keep the lip corners loose. Then read through your text, speaking in the accent as if there is numbing agent in the lip corners. Allow for this sensation to encourage the corners to release and let go. Check your mouth in a small hand-held mirror to be sure the lip corners aren't stuck in one position as you transition to speaking at a normal speed.

The tongue is sitting too low

When the tongue sits too low, it will affect the main vowel sounds, as well as impacting the primary consonant in the American accent: the consonant R. The American tongue sits a bit higher than many British regional accents, so this could be an area to explore in your own practice. In fact, it could feel as if the inside of your mouth needs to be 'smaller' or more 'squished' in the American accent when pronouncing the consonant R.

A low tongue along with a dropped jaw may lead to the vowel before R sounding hollow. Listen specifically to the vowel and R combination in words such as: BIRD, WORD, NURSE, TURN (▶ 3.6). Compare your pronunciation with that of a native speaker. If it seems different, it may be an indicator that the tongue is sitting too low. Return to the High Tongue Position exercise.

The jaw is becoming overly involved

When an actor seems to be overworking the muscles of speech, the accent can begin to feel false to the audience. One area where this occurs is the jaw, which can tighten unnecessarily as you move other muscles in your mouth.

The jaw is a prime place to hold excess tension, but we don't want that to come into play for the American accent. You can check your own jaw in a hand-held mirror. Return to the Jaw Release exercise when necessary.

The accent sounds overly nasal or lacks nasality

If the accent is overly nasal it may be due to the soft palate resting too low, which allows for sound to travel up through the nose. Return to the Soft Palate Yawn Stretch warm-up to encourage a shift. It may also be a question of resonance, which is explored later in Chapter 3: The Music.

If the accent lacks nasality, it may be due to the soft palate sitting too high on the American nasal sounds AN and AM. Return to Nasality Practice to troubleshoot.

Finally...

The mouth's setting is the physical foundation of any accent. These exercises help reground and recentre your accent, so refer back to them at any time. Just as you warm up at the gym, so too can you use this chapter as a basis for warming up your American accent.

2. The Sounds

There are a lot of anatomical descriptions throughout this chapter to guide you through the sounds of the American accent. If visualising anatomy is useful to you, that's great. If not, there are links to audio files throughout, and I encourage you to listen to the sounds in order to practise by repeating these sounds aloud. Learning by ear is just as useful as learning by feel or by sight, so use the different options to find a learning style that works best for you.

These are the most important sounds to develop when speaking in the General American accent. They are explored in detail in this chapter:

Consonants	Vowels	The Details
R L T	TR<u>A</u>P and B<u>A</u>TH L<u>O</u>T and TH<u>OU</u>GHT G<u>O</u>AT	C<u>U</u>P and WH<u>A</u>T TH <u>T</u>UNE and <u>NEW</u> BEEN

The Consonant R

The consonant R is a good place to start your work on the General American accent because it is a *rhotic accent*, meaning that the consonant R is pronounced every time it is written in a word.

Identify if you already pronounce the consonant R every time it is written in a word by reading the list of words below out loud in your own voice. Many speakers from England, for example, may not pronounce a consonant R unless it is followed directly by a vowel. These speakers will find that while there *is* a sound made in place of the underlined R, it will most likely be a vowel and not an actual consonant R.

▶ 3.1

lette<u>r</u>	fo<u>r</u>ce	squa<u>re</u>	bi<u>r</u>d
sta<u>r</u>t	no<u>r</u>th	nea<u>r</u>	nu<u>r</u>se

You may find that you *do* pronounce the consonant R. There are certainly other rhotic accents besides General American: Scottish and Irish accents, for example.

What is an R?

The consonant R sound is made by contracting the muscles of the tongue and moving the tongue into a position that partially blocks airflow. No contraction or movement of the tongue equals no R!

There are many different ways to make the consonant R which can differ between accents. Be aware that the way you pronounce the consonant R might not necessarily be the same as how an American would pronounce an R. Hear the many ways the consonant R is pronounced in a variety of languages and accents below.

Making Many Types of Rs

Try these Rs out on the following sentence. Use the recording as a guide.

The very high price on red runner's shorts are horribly raised and should be a crime.

1. TRILL the tip of the tongue into an R
   The tip of the tongue comes up behind the front teeth and continually flaps against the gum ridge to make a trill. This is common in Spanish and Italian speakers and is sometimes called a 'rolling R'.

2. TAP the tip of the tongue into an R
   The tip of the tongue comes up behind the teeth and very quickly taps the gum ridge to form an R. This may be heard in speakers from parts of Scotland and Wales.

3. BEND the tip of the tongue into an R
   The tip of the tongue lifts up behind the teeth and then drops without touching any other part of the inside of the mouth. It may feel as if the tongue tip is gently bending backwards. This is very typical of the Received Pronunciation accent

4. RETROFLEX the tip of the tongue into an R
   This is an extreme version of the Bend R, where the

tip of the tongue curls back into a flex towards the roof of the mouth. This R may be heard in many Irish accents.

5. TRILL the uvula into an R
   The uvula can be described as the little dangly bit in the back of your mouth. Move your focus to the back of the tongue. Allow the back of the tongue to rise up and trill the uvula. This R could also be described as the Chewbacca sound, and can be achieved through gargling water. This R is used in French and German languages.

6. SUBSTITUTE a W for an R
   Some speakers may not make an R at all, but instead push their lips forward into a W as a substitute to make an R. You can hear this from the classic Looney Tunes character, Elmer Fudd, when he talks about 'wascally wabbits'.

   Many speakers of contemporary London English may find that they too substitute a W for an R sound albeit in a more subtle way by using the lips as the primary action to make an R. In this case, speakers with an R substitution should work to find muscularity in their tongue in order to produce the American R.

7. BUNCH the back of the tongue to form an R
   The Bunched R is the basis of the General American consonant R. Let's look at how to bunch next:

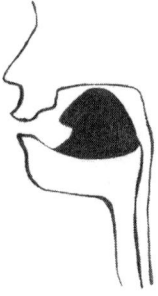

Mastering the General American R

In the General American accent, R is made through a unique bunching and lifting action of the back of the tongue. To practise making this sound:

1. The back of the tongue bunches together as if you were making the fibres at the back of your tongue thick like a sausage.
2. The tongue pulls back and lifts up as if you were swallowing.
3. The sides of the tongue may brace against the inside of the upper molars in order to gain a bit of traction to help this action.
4. It may feel as if the body of the tongue is winding up.
5. And, most importantly of all, the entire action is rather quick and springlike.

Return back to the High Tongue Position 1 exercise to explore this in action.

Initial Practice

The tongue is an important part of the American accent, as it directly affects the pronunciation of the consonant R.

In the accent the middle and back of the tongue engage to create the sound, not the front of the tongue. It may feel as if the action shifts to the back of the tongue.

1. Bring your tongue outside of your mouth so that the tongue rests on your bottom lip. Allow for a sense of release through the entire tongue.
2. Keeping your tongue down on your bottom lip outside of your mouth, read the following sentence aloud:

   Rachel had a hard start to the race, but she got better over time and won the prize fair and square.

3. Feel the middle back of the tongue engaging to form the Rs. Keep the tip of your tongue resting down throughout this exercise.
4. Then place your tongue back in the mouth. Repeat the same sentence, but keep the sense of action in the back of your tongue, similar to when you had it out of your mouth.

Don't worry about sounding silly when the tongue is out of your mouth. Focus instead on the sensations happening in the mouth to form the bunched R.

Five R-Vowel Combinations

To move your practice forward, you should practise the consonant R in the context you'll experience it when performing. It's all well and good to practise the American R as a purely anatomical pursuit as described above, but you need to begin using the R within words so that you can employ the American R with ease when speaking.

The five R-Vowel Combinations are a guide for your practice because they consist of all of the ways you can experience the R after a vowel in this American accent.

Remember, this guide is for a non-regional General American accent. Individual American speakers may differ due to regionalisms and idiosyncrasies.

The American R is unique because it can feel like it attaches itself to the preceding vowel. It may even seem as if the R has wrapped itself around the vowel it follows. Linguists call this phenomenon 'R colouration'. Think of the American R as if it's fused or glued to the vowel before it, not separate.

3.5

R	Phonetic Symbols	Example Words Based on the Kit List
ER	ɚ / ɝ	LETTER & NURSE
OR	ɔɚ	FORCE & NORTH
AR	ɑɚ	START & CAR
AIR	eɚ	SQUARE & FAIR
EER	ɪɚ	NEAR & CHEER

Notice that the only thing that changes in each combination is the vowel. So even though there are different vowels preceding the R, the actual consonant R is pronounced the same.

To practise, visualise beginning with the vowel and then gliding your tongue into the sound ER /ɚ/ as in LETTER. Feel the consonant R connected to the vowel sound. This glide action gives the sensation of binding the vowel to the R as if they are happening together.

Keep in mind that the American R is rather short. There can be a tendency to overdo the sound to be sure it's pronounced. Keep the R quick and place any extra energy into the vowel preceding the R instead.

| ER | ɚ / ɜ˞ | LETTER & NURSE |

▶ 3.6

I call this sound the 'Favourite American R' because it comes up so often in the American accent. There are three main places where you will use ER /ɚ/ as in LETTER.

1. It appears in words that *end in -ER* and other spellings of the unstressed R syllable (e.g. -re, -ar, -or). Even though there are different vowels preceding the R, all of these word endings are pronounced the same. This R is quite quick and short in its pronunciation.

    smaller   letter   figure   beggar   visor

2. R also appears in the middle of words in an *unstressed syllable*.

    neighbourhood   government   butternut
    brotherhood   exercise

3. Finally, this sound is heard in the middle of words in a *stressed syllable*, such as the word NURSE.

    This vowel may seem slightly longer than the words listed above in 1 and 2. This is because this R is in a stressed syllable. But when speaking quickly this vowel is very similar to the sound described above in 2, so I've combined these for practical purposes.

b<u>ir</u>d   w<u>or</u>d   h<u>ear</u>d   v<u>er</u>dict   n<u>ur</u>se

Helpful Hint: Remember that English as a language does not pronounce words phonetically. This means that words are not pronounced according to how they are spelled. There may be a range of spelling options that correspond with the same desired sound, just like in the General American pronunciation of Mary, merry and marry.

Practice Sentences

The customer is at the centre of a major internal error.

We searched over the entire Earth to find the person responsible for the work.

The colonel murdered the girl for her pearls.
(*The first syllable in colonel is pronounced with a consonant R in the General American accent, like ker'nl.*)

Those teenagers were forever gathering early at the church on the other side of Denver.

Text Practice

Cynthia from Sweat *by Lynn Nottage*

❝You know Brucie, he can be as smooth as satin. T<u>ur</u>n that shit on and off at the drop of a dime. Things w<u>er</u>e going fine, then Christmas Day, we've got this nice bottle of Chablis. He's looking dapp<u>er</u>. I'm dressed for dang<u>er</u>. We'<u>re</u> laughing, chilling and having fun. And… we talk. I mean, talk. It's all good. We drink wine, we drink some more wine, then we do what you do aft<u>er</u> you drink too much wine.

Jess from Cost of Living *by Martyna Majok*

❝ And the n<u>ur</u>se asks my mom like, what'll you call h<u>er</u>? And my mom just looks at h<u>er</u>. She said that's the moment it hit h<u>er</u>, how alone she is. How little English. How everything now it's h<u>ers</u>. H<u>er</u> should<u>ers</u>. And she thought the n<u>ur</u>se said — When my mom was asked a question, she'd usually eith<u>er</u> just say yes or no or okay like judgin on if it was a man or a woman she was answ<u>er</u>in...

OR	ɔɚ	FORCE & NORTH

▶ 3.7

Explore the sound:

1. Round your lips into the shape of a small circle and bring the body of your tongue towards the back of your mouth. It may feel as if the body of your tongue is sitting directly under the soft palate.

2. Then release your lips to the side to form a slight smile as you bunch the tongue back and up into the American R. This is a quick movement.

Try the sound in a word:

f<u>or</u>ce   n<u>or</u>th   c<u>our</u>se   b<u>or</u>ed   Calif<u>or</u>nia

The following words in a General American accent also use OR /ɔɚ/ as in F<u>OR</u>CE. Be sure to keep the vowel sound the same, even if in your accent the sound differs:

f<u>o</u>reign   h<u>o</u>rrible   <u>o</u>range   h<u>o</u>roscope   f<u>o</u>rest

Practice Sentences ▶ 3.7

We will use torture or force only as a last resort.

The warrior stood before his wardrobe door in order to find her sword.

It's horribly adorable to give horoscope advice to a Californian orange.

Text Practice

Zack from Belleville *by Amy Herzog*

❝ It's t<u>or</u>ture. But I'm not allowed to say anything because that would be unsupp<u>or</u>tive. And this is a period of transition. Meanwhile I'm thinking of res<u>or</u>ting to mashing them up in her food, it's just… so not a good idea.

| **AR** | ɑɚ | **ST<u>AR</u>T & C<u>AR</u>** |

Explore the sound:

1. Open your mouth, as if saying AH at the doctor's office.

2. Allow your tongue to sit low and back in the mouth. It may even feel as if you are cupping a small coin on the back of your tongue. The target sound is AH /ɑ/ as in SP<u>A</u>.

3. Then bring the mouth slightly more closed as you engage the back of your tongue to rise and bunch into R.

Try the sound in a word:

f<u>ar</u>m   c<u>ar</u>   st<u>ar</u>t   h<u>ar</u>d   p<u>ar</u>k

Practice Sentences

As far as I'm concerned, the partying has gone too far.

He's barking mad if he thinks he can park the car near the farmer's yard.

She's an absolute martyr for darning the socks with yarn.

Text Practice

Kathy from Clybourne Park *by Bruce Norris*

❝ And if the Landm<u>ar</u>ks Committee really wants to pick that fight with the Zoning Dep<u>ar</u>tment that is their business, but that's a matter of if and when.

Helpful Hint: Be careful not to rely overly on the front of your tongue to make the consonant R. If you do, AR /ɑɚ/ as in START will start to sound like a pirate! Instead focus on bunching and lifting up the back of your tongue to make the R. Always remember to spring out of the sound at the end so that the R is short and quick.

AIR	eə	SQUARE & FAIR

Explore the sound:

1. Begin the sound with your mouth half open and your tongue forward in the mouth.

2. The target starting vowel is EH /e/ as in DR<u>E</u>SS, but with your tongue a little higher in your mouth.

3. Then bunch your tongue back and up into R.

4. It may feel as if there is a silent Y /j/ as in <u>Y</u>ES hiding between the two sounds through the transition.

Try the sound in a word:

squ<u>are</u>   f<u>air</u>   sh<u>are</u>   b<u>ear</u>   wh<u>ere</u>

The following words in a General American accent also use AIR /eə/ as in SQU<u>A</u>RE.

<u>Pa</u>ris   <u>ca</u>rry   emb<u>a</u>rrass   <u>ma</u>rry   <u>pa</u>rents

Helpful Hint: If your tongue begins too high or low in the mouth you will start on the wrong vowel and the resulting AIR /eə/ as in SQU<u>A</u>RE won't end up sounding exactly right. Finding the 'sweet spot' is key.

Practice Sentences

Mary got married and she was very merry.
(*Yes, they're all pronounced the same!*)

The bear put some pear in his hair and called it self-care.

We won the d_are_, f_air_ and squ_are_.

Text Practice

Joanne from Company *by Stephen Sondheim and George Furth*

❝ It's the little things you sh_are_ together,
Sw_ear_ together,
B_ear_ together,
That make perfect relationships.

EER	ɪə	NEAR & CHEER

Explore the sound:

1. Begin the sound on the vowel IH /ɪ/ as in K<u>I</u>T.

2. Then bunch your tongue back and up into R.

3. It may feel as if there is a silent Y /j/ as in <u>Y</u>ES helping to move your tongue between the two sounds during the move.

Try the sound in a word:

ne_ar_   fe_ar_   che_er_   be_er_   de_ar_

Practice Sentences

Be of good cheer, dear!

The cashier was sincere when ringing up the price of beer.

Seriously, the experience was a spiritual miracle.

Text Practice

Jess from Cost of Living *by Martyna Majok*

“My mother came to the country with no English, very little, and she's in this hospital in Newark – it's not there anymore this is cl<u>ear</u>ly like a few y<u>ear</u>s – and the nurse hands me to my mom for the first time.

R Drills

It is imperative to drill the consonant R so that it becomes second nature in your mouth, and later embeds itself into your entire voice and body. Keep your breathing open and free throughout the following exercises so that the sound can become fully embodied and not isolated at the level of the mouth. You may even want to move around the room as you practise aloud.

Also be sure to keep the R short and quick as you practise. The biggest mistake you can make, besides not pronouncing the R, is *overpronouncing* the R. Think of the action as a trampoline, with the tongue bouncing into an R and then launching out of it. This springy launch will allow you to move easily into the next word or syllable instead of trapping you in the R. An actor I worked with likened it to an ocean wave, with the tongue pulling into the wave and then releasing as the 'wave' (your tongue) washes ashore.

The goal is to find the right amount of tension in the tongue to make the R. If the tongue doesn't move into the R, you will miss the R entirely and end up pronouncing a vowel. This may end up sounding like a stereotypical New York City accent. But too much tension in the tongue will lead to the R sounding overworked and false, so you must be careful not to overexert the tongue.

The General American R Workout

This exercise has been adapted from Cicely Berry's book *Voice and the Actor*.

1. Begin by reading down the first column, practising the ER /ɚ/ as in LETT<u>ER</u> and /ɜ˞/ NU<u>R</u>SE.
2. Then read the second column, practising OR /ɔɚ/ as in F<u>OR</u>CE.
3. Then read the third column, practising AR /ɑɚ/ as in ST<u>AR</u>T.
4. Then read the fourth column, practising AIR /eɚ/ as in SQU<u>ARE</u>.
5. Finally, read the fifth column, practising EER /ɪɚ/ as in NEA<u>R</u>.

Take care that your tongue and jaw do not drop too low when practising these sounds, as that will lead to the vowel before the R sounding hollow. Return to the exercise in Initial Practice any time to reset your tongue and recentre yourself in the American R.

▶ 3.11

You'll notice that there are two lines that start with TH. This is because there are two TH sounds in English, one voiced and the other unvoiced. The voiced TH is made with the breath and the unvoiced TH is made with vibration. TH is pronounced with the tongue tip almost touching the back of the teeth or with the tongue slightly between the teeth. The breath TH appears in words like THIN, THINK and MONTH. The voiced TH will feel like vibration on the back of your teeth and appears in words like THEM, THESE and MOTHER.

ER /ə/ LETTER	OR /ɔə/ FORCE	AR /ɑə/ START	AIR /eə/ SQUARE	EER /ɪə/ NEAR
PER	POR	PAR	PAIR	PEER
BER	BOR	BAR	BAIR	BEER
MER	MOR	MAR	MAIR	MEER
TER	TOR	TAR	TAIR	TEER
DER	DOR	DAR	DAIR	DEER
NER	NOR	NAR	NAIR	NEER
KER	KOR	KAR	KAIR	KEER
GER	GOR	GAR	GAIR	GEER
FER	FOR	FAR	FAIR	FEER

ER /ɚ/ LETT**ER**	OR /ɔɚ/ F**OR**CE	AR /ɑɚ/ ST**AR**T	AIR /eɚ/ SQU**ARE**	EER /ɪɚ/ N**EAR**
VER	VOR	VAR	VAIR	VEER
SER	SOR	SAR	SAIR	SEER
ZER	ZOR	ZAR	ZAIR	ZEER
THER	THOR	THAR	THAIR	THEER
THER	THOR	THAR	THAIR	THEER
LER	LOR	LAR	LAIR	LEER

The next exercise is similar, but now the consonant appears after R. Return to thinking of the R as if on a trampoline: first pronouncing the R before bouncing off of it into the consonant that follows. In simpler terms, the R is pronounced but it is short and quick.

3.12

ER /ə/ LETTER	OR /ɔə/ FORCE	AR /ɑə/ START	AIR /eə/ SQUARE	EER /ɪə/ NEAR
ERP	ORP	ARP	AIRP	EERP
ERB	ORB	ARB	AIRB	EERB
ERM	ORM	ARM	AIRM	EERM
ERT	ORT	ART	AIRT	EERT
ERD	ORD	ARD	AIRD	EERD
ERN	ORN	ARN	AIRN	EERN
ERK	ORK	ARK	AIRK	EERK
ERG	ORG	ARG	AIRG	EERG
ERF	ORF	ARF	AIRF	EERF
ERV	ORV	ARV	AIRV	EERV
ERS	ORS	ARS	AIRS	EERS
ERZ	ORZ	ARZ	AIRZ	EERZ
ERTH	ORTH	ARTH	AIRTH	EERTH
ERTH	ORTH	ARTH	AIRTH	EERTH
ERL	ORL	ARL	AIRL	EERL

The General American R Workout 2

Once the General American R Workout becomes easier, you can practise going across the rows, switching the vowel sound as you go.

→	ERP	ORP	ARP	AIRP	EERP
→	ERB	ORB	ARB	AIRB	EERB
→	ERM	ORM	ARM	AIRM	EERM

…and so on. This will train your ability to switch between the sounds with ease.

Text Practice

Once you understand the basics of R, it's time to practise it on text. This is the most important stage of the work, but a stage that is so often neglected. I regularly encounter actors who have never practised the target sound aloud on text – and those who do often practise silently or on a whisper. The more you bring your full voice to the accent through text exploration, the quicker you will feel confident using the accent in performance.

Always practise one sound change at a time in order to feel in control and not overwhelmed. The following exercise specifically focuses on the consonant R. This is the time to get a handle on moving between the five R-Vowel Combinations in speech with ease. I have included two passages below. Each R sound has been highlighted above the word.

Prior from Angels in America, Part One *by Tony Kushner*

>   AR   EER ER   ER
> "Look. G<u>ar</u>lic. A mi<u>rr</u>or. Holy Wat<u>er</u>. A crucifix. FUCK OFF! Get the fuck out of my room! GO!"

Practise the Rs out of context first before building up to the entire line:

1.	AR	EER	ER	ER
2.	GAR	MEER	ER	DER
3.	GAR	MEER	RER	DER
4.	GARLIC	MIR–	–RER	WATER

       Garlic.   A mirror.   Holy Water.

Then practise the consonant in a longer passage. I have underlined when the consonant R appears in the text below. I have also designated which of the five R-Vowel Combinations is the correct choice above the word. Notice that the spelling of the word does not necessarily correspond with the target sound. This is because pronunciations may differ from the word spelling, as explained before.

As you begin, I encourage you to focus on one sound change at a time. For this exercise just focus on the consonant R when practising the text. I encourage you to mark your script like I've done below if you find the consonant R tricky. As you get more advanced, you will be able to remember more than one sound change at a time.

Harper from Angels in America, Part Two *by Tony Kushner*

❝ Night flight to San Francisco; chase the moon across
    AIR   EER
America. God! It's been years since I was on a plane!
            ER
When we hit thirty-five-thousand feet, we'll have
reached the tropopause. The great belt of calm air. As
     ER
close as I'll ever get to the ozone.

                ER.   AIR
I dreamed we were there. The plane leapt the
                   AIR   ER
tropopause, the safe air, and attained the outer rim,
                                   OR
the ozone, which was ragged and torn, patches of it
   AIR
threadbare as old cheesecloth, and that was
frightening…
But I saw something only I could see, because of my
astonishing ability to see such things:

                 ER.   AR
Souls were rising, from the earth far below, souls of
                    AIR
the dead, of people who had perished, from famine,
 OR
from war, from the plague, and they floated up, like
 ER   ER
skydivers in reverse, limbs all akimbo, wheeling and
                            AR
spinning. And the souls of these departed joined
                      OR
hands, clasped ankles, and formed a web, a great net
               ER
of souls, and the souls were three-atom oxygen
                                 ER
molecules, of the stuff of ozone, and the outer rim
 OR   AIR
absorbed them, and was repaired.

Nothing's lost foreve<u>r</u>. In this wo<u>r</u>ld, there is a kind of
      ER   ER

painful progress. Longing fo<u>r</u> what we've left behind,
            OR

and dreaming ahead. At least I think that's so.

Troubleshooting

R before S

Take care always to pronounce the consonant R before the letter S, such as in plurals or possessives. To do this:

1. Feel your tongue move into the American R.

2. Your tongue tip can also rise up into a quick flick in order to bring R and S together seamlessly.

3. Then feel your tongue move into position to pronounce the letter S. Usually your tongue tip is pointing up behind your front teeth, but some may find that their tongue ends in a tongue tip down position, and this is also fine.

4. Take care not to get stuck in a SH /ʃ/ sound, or the consonants will sound slushy and slurred together.

It may feel at first that pronouncing R before an S slows down your speech, but with practice you will train yourself to do it at speed.

Practice Sentences

The two sisters wrote many letters over the years to their brothers.

Anders owns four pairs of runner's trousers.

The kindergartners read two chapters of the school director's book.

R in unstressed syllables

It is easy to become so focused on pronouncing consonant R that you end up stressing a syllable that should be unstressed. Just because the consonant R is pronounced does not mean that syllable is stressed. Otherwise, it may lead to some very interesting pronunciations!

Keep the stress on the correct syllable when practising.

▶ 3.15

weather	<u>WEA</u>ther ✔	wea<u>THER</u> ✘
commuter	com<u>MU</u>ter ✔	commu<u>TER</u> ✘
government	<u>GO</u>Vernment ✔	go<u>VER</u>nment ✘
procrastinator	pro<u>CRAS</u>tinator ✔	procrastina<u>TOR</u> ✘

Avoid intrusive Rs

Up to this point you have worked on pronouncing an R every time it is written in a word. In the General American accent, the consonant R is only pronounced when the letter is written in the word. You shouldn't add one when there is no R written.

Keep an eye on words that end in -a, like in ARE<u>A</u> or REBECC<u>A</u>. In your own accent this vowel may be pronounced the same as words ending in -er, like MOTH<u>ER</u>. In a General American accent, the pronunciations will differ depending on if a letter R is present or not.

Words Ending in R	**Words Ending in A**
lette<u>r</u> close<u>r</u>	id<u>ea</u> comm<u>a</u>

Avoiding adding a linking R or intrusive R to words like those in the second column. A linking R is a consonant R that slips its way between 2 vowel sounds to create a bridge between the two words. This is sometimes also called an intrusive R.

> Pizza(r) and chips
>
> India(r) and China
>
> Rebecca(r) and me
>
> Sofa(r) in the room

A linking R does *not* happen in a General American accent!

The American accent puts a *glottal* between the two vowel sounds instead. A glottal is made when the vocal folds come together to block the airflow before lightly exploding apart. You can feel this if you gently hold your hand to your throat and say 'Uh oh!' This may feel like:

> [airflow stop] UH [airflow stop] OH

Begin by substituting the letter H between the words, which will make the glottal action easier. Focus on keeping the mouth fully open and the tongue resting down between the vowels in this exercise.

Pizza (*keep mouth open and tongue down*) Hand chips

India (*keep mouth open and tongue down*) Hand China

Rebecca (*keep mouth open and tongue down*) Hand me

Sofa (*keep mouth open and tongue down*) Hin the room

Next, transition to a glottal by removing the H between the words. You can think of the H as silent in the next exercise. Continue to be mindful of keeping the mouth open and the tongue resting down in the mouth between the two vowels. You may even feel like you are making a little bounce across the two words.

Pizza (*bounce*) and chips

India (*bounce*) and China

Rebecca (*bounce*) and me

Sofa (*bounce*) in the room

Practice Sentences

America is famous for its pizza and hamburgers.

The idea of being in Florida in August sounds terrible to Lydia and me.

Let me tell you the saga about Donna and me after a few too many vodka on the rocks.

Mouth check-in

Occasionally, actors overly round their lips when pronouncing the American R. Whilst a bit of lip rounding is fine, you do not want this sound to be overly shaped at the front of the mouth. Instead, the main action should exist in the middle and back of the tongue. The tongue is the leader here – not your lips.

You can practise this by placing your index finger vertically on your lips, resting just under your nose. As you practise the following words, encourage the lips to release and the tongue to lead the action. Allow yourself to feel the lips releasing under your finger. It may even feel as if the tongue is winding up on each R.

reason   river   rabbit   rough   riding   rain

As previously, I encourage you to use a small hand-held mirror or a smartphone camera on selfie mode in order to see your mouth and check in with its shape throughout the exercises. You can also return to the exercise in Initial Practice at the beginning of the chapter to release and reset your tongue.

Moving Forward...

The consonant R is one of the most important and often toughest consonants to master in the American accent. As you move forward with the remaining vowels and consonants, you can always refer back to this chapter for routine top-up practice. The muscles of your mouth and face are very small in size. Because of this, new speech movement patterns can lose strength and precision if not worked out on a regular basis. I encourage you to revisit the American R for continuing practice so that the muscles respond appropriately and easily to make the sound in performance.

The Consonant L

The General American accent uses a *velarised L* each time the consonant L appears in a word. This means that the back of the tongue lifts up towards the soft palate. This action is also referred to as a 'dark L'. It may feel like you are gently swallowing while pronouncing the consonant L, as if the L is focused towards the back of the mouth. This action is used for L at the beginning, in the middle, or at the end of a word in this American accent.

In accent work, the consonant L can be considered a close relative to the consonant R. When I say that R and L are 'related', this is because both of these consonants are *approximates*. An approximate is a consonant made by bringing one part of the mouth close to another without causing audible friction or a stop in the airflow. Because approximates are very similar to vowel sounds, they tend to change shape from accent to accent.

In a General American accent, the consonant R has a similar physical action to the consonant L. In this case, both consonants take on a bunching action at the back of the tongue.

▶ 4.1

Initial L	Middle L (L before a vowel)	Final L (L after a vowel)
love	follow	will
lady	really	school
leap	elephant	feel
library	knowledge	oval
laughable	zoology	boil

Mastering the Velarised L

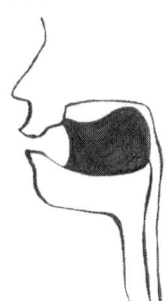

The velarised L is made through a bunching and lifting action at the back of the tongue whilst the tongue tip rests on the gum ridge. To practise making this sound:

1. The tip of the tongue rises up to touch the gum ridge behind the teeth.
2. The tip of the tongue exerts a slight pressure on the gum ridge to help raise the back of the tongue.
3. Keep the tongue tip on the gum ridge as the back of the tongue bunches together. It may feel as if you are making the fibres at the back of your tongue thick like a sausage.

4. This action should equally lift up the back of the tongue as if you were swallowing.
5. The tongue tip stays resting on the gum ridge until the sound is completed.
6. And, most importantly of all, the entire action with the back of the tongue is quick and springlike.

Initial Practice

In this accent, the middle and back of the tongue will engage to create the consonant L.

1. Bring your tongue outside of your mouth so that the tongue rests on your bottom lip. Allow for a sense of release through the entire tongue.
2. Keeping your tongue flat on your bottom lip outside of your mouth, read the following sentence aloud:

   Recently police learned that Larry stole millions of dollars from the hospital.

3. Feel the middle and back of the tongue engaging in a bunching action to form the Ls. Keep the tip of the tongue resting flat throughout this exercise.
4. Then place the tongue back in the mouth. Repeat the same sentence but keep the sense of action in the back of the tongue that you felt when you had the tongue out of the mouth.

Continuing Practice

Practise pronouncing the consonant L in different positions in a word. Use this back-focused velarised L each time the consonant L appears.

will — leave

all — luck

itself — long

help — Louise

available — locker

professional — class

hospital — lab

grateful — lover

lost — television

large — watermelon

jungle — elephant

Practice Sentences

L at the Beginning of a Word

Liam looks a lot like his sister Lucy.

Let's look at that problem later.

Lydia leaned in and laughed loudly.

L Before a Vowel

> They freely follow the leader of the cult.
>
> I put eleven dollars in my wallet before I left the house.
>
> My family doesn't like olives, but we love melon.

L Towards the End of a Word

> Are you available to call her at twelve o'clock?
>
> A successful judicial clerk is practical and professional.
>
> The terrible football team lost because they were too physical on the field.

Text Practice

Dean from Gloria *by Branden Jacobs-Jenkins*

❝ I can only seem to recall it in bits and pieces – and putting it all together has really forced me to reflect a lot on that time and myself and who I was... back then... before Gloria, and I've kind of come to this conclusion that maybe I wasn't... the best guy... that I was an asshole basically – which might have something to do with that environment – but also you know I was drinking a lot and sort of unhappy with where I was in my life and only kind of realizing this – and, anyway, it's just, it has all kind of led me to this place of really wanting to apologize to you... for anything I might have said that hurt your feelings or anything like that –

Troubleshooting

There are variations to pronouncing the consonant L between languages and accents. It is useful to first understand how you pronounce the consonant L in your own accent. From there, you can use that knowledge to then master the velarised L.

The key to making a successful velarised L is for the tip of the tongue to touch the gum ridge whilst the back of the tongue is engaging in a bunch-and-lift action. Ultimately, the action in the back of your tongue helps to create the sound. It may feel as if you are gently swallowing your tongue when producing the sound.

You can troubleshoot depending on the following circumstances:

The back of the tongue is not engaging

In some accents only the tongue tip is involved in the action making the consonant L. The tip of the tongue comes up to meet the gum ridge behind the teeth, but the back of the tongue does not engage. This is sometimes referred to as the 'clear L' or the 'light L', and may be heard in accents from Ireland, Wales, and many Western European languages such as French, Italian and German.

To make a velarised L (or 'dark L') for the General American accent, the action should be towards the middle and back of the tongue. Rest the tip of the tongue on the gum ridge as the back of the tongue engages. You can visualise trying to make the consonant G at the same time to help lift your tongue. Hold this position until the preceding vowel. It may feel as if the velarised L is held for longer than the clear L.

The lips are rounding forward as a substitute for the tongue

The tip of the tongue may not rise to meet the gum ridge for many speakers of English. Instead, the consonant L is made by slightly rounding the lips. This is usually heard at the end of words and can be found in certain accents from England. Speak the words below in front of a mirror and see if your lips are rounding as a substitute for the tongue:

belt   able   full   bottle

For General American, take care that the tip of the tongue is coming up to meet the gum ridge each time you pronounce the consonant L. Rest a finger on the lips to feel if they are rounding forward. The action should be occurring predominantly in your tongue rather than in your lips.

The back of the tongue is engaging too much

It can be that the back of the tongue is engaging too much, creating an overly swallowed sensation in the root of the tongue. It may even feel as if the back of the tongue is being swallowed with some force.

Although there is some engagement in the back of the tongue in the American velarised L, it is important to find that 'sweet spot' so that the L does not become too swallowed in the throat. The focus point of the action needs to change in order to transition to the American velarised L. Sense the middle of the tongue is contracting, not the tongue root. Visualise the tongue further forward in your mouth. You can also imagine that the action is quick and light as you practise.

I encourage you to warm up using the tongue exercises found in Chapter 1: The Mouth. For example, you can speak a practice text with the tongue resting on the bottom lip outside of the mouth in order to sense a release in the tongue. Targeted exercises will help support release of your tongue root.

The Consonant T

The consonant T could be called the chameleon of the General American accent because it may not always be pronounced as you might expect. In fact, the consonant T changes depending on the position it appears in a word: at the beginning, in the middle between vowels, or at the end.

In most English accents, the consonant T is pronounced by bringing the tongue tip up to the gum ridge behind the front teeth. The tongue stops the airflow for a moment before releasing from that position, making the consonant T, usually with a small puff of air – or aspiration – to accompany it.

This chapter focuses on the consonant T in the middle and at the end of a word. This is because the consonant T changes pronunciations in these positions in an American accent.

▶ 5.1

Initial T	Middle T	Final T
take	letter	get
talent	pretty	what
Tom	water	hot
telephone	computer	accredit
truth	little	apart

T in the Middle of a Word

The consonant T in the middle of a word changes to become what may feel like a very quick D. This is called a 'flap T' or a 'tap T', and is made by the tip of the tongue as it quickly leaves the gum ridge. It may feel as if your tongue is making a quick flutter action as it rises and falls quickly after touching the gum ridge. This action is similar to rolling the tip of your tongue for one single roll. An actor once described this as the tongue tip giving the gum ridge a high-five.

Finding the Middle T

▶ 5.2

1. Begin by trilling or blowing your tongue tip as in Rrrr.
2. Then slow down the tongue rolling until you are isolating one single roll at a time. This is a tap.

Alternatively:

1. If you can't trill or roll your tongue, begin by making the consonant D.

2. Then add in a vowel sound between making the consonant D, alternating between the vowel and the consonant.

     a-duh a-duh a-duh a-duh

3. Begin to speed this sound up. At quick speeds your tongue will be making a tap.

4. You can also alternate between a consonant T and a consonant D. Similar to above, at quick speeds your tongue will be making a tap.

     tuh-duh-tuh-duh-tuh-duh

Practice Sentences

The firefighter's daughter is a writer.

We water the tomatoes on Saturday.

There are little butterflies all over the city.

I'm pretty sure that Peter has the water bottle.

It doesn't matter if the rider is getting thirsty.

Exceptions to the Rule

Rules are made to be broken, and this rule is no exception. If the consonant T is at the beginning of a *stressed syllable*, the T in the middle of a word will be pronounced like an initial T. It will not change actions like it does above.

However, do not allow the T to become too percussive, like a snare drum. You can avoid this by keeping the tongue tip broad on the gum ridge.

| ta<u>tt</u>oo | pre<u>t</u>end | gui<u>tar</u> | four<u>teen</u> |
| a<u>tt</u>ack | i<u>ta</u>lics | ho<u>t</u>el | po<u>ta</u>to |

Helpful Hint: In the word *potato*, the first T is pronounced, and the second is a quick tap.

Practice Sentences

> The hotel has seventeen rooms.
>
> Do all guitar players have tattoos?
>
> He's pretending to protect himself from attack.
>
> The Canadian dentist's dog likes to go on walks in the daytime.

T at the End of a Word

When the consonant T appears at the end of a word, it can sometimes feel unfinished or unpronounced in an American accent. Instead of releasing the tongue from the gum ridge to finish the word, a *glottal stop* is often created behind the tongue.

As explored before, a glottal is made when the vocal folds come together to block the airflow before lightly exploding apart. Remind yourself of this feeling by gently holding your hand to your throat and saying 'Uh oh!' This may feel like:

[airflow stop] UH [airflow stop] OH

Finding the Glottal T

1. Bring your tongue tip up to the gum ridge as if making a consonant T.
2. Keep your tongue tip on the gum ridge as you say 'Uh oh' with your tongue in place on the ridge.
3. This practises your ability to create a glottal with your tongue tip up on the gum ridge.

Then transition this exercise into speaking words:

1. Start with the word 'hot'. Bring your tongue tip up to the gum ridge as if making the consonant T at the end of the word.
2. Once your tongue tip is on the gum ridge, stop the airflow momentarily. This small stop in airflow creates a glottal in place of the consonant T.

Practice Sentences

I hate being apart from my friend.

I don't have much faith in what's going on out there.

I don't want that.

Exceptions to the Rule

The consonant T can also feel like a very quick D when a vowel starts the following word. This is the 'flap T' referred to in the section: T in the Middle of a Word. This sound is made by the tip of your tongue as it quickly leaves the gum ridge. It may even feel as if it's connecting the two words together.

hot_outside   pot_of gold   cheat_and steal

Practice Sentences

A lot of weight is put on the table.

Get out of the way before you get in the car.

Sit at the foot of the bed.

Helpful Hint: Sometimes a speaker will create a glottal T in this position instead of using the flap. It all depends on the context, how quickly the person is speaking, and what flows best. You may need to make your own judgements based on the text and then adjust for clarity. Both choices are correct, but one may be preferable depending on the circumstances.

Not every T is changed into a glottal stop or a flap at the end of a word. Sometimes a T can be used for emphasis at the end of a word, if it is being stressed or to indicate emotion behind the word.

Practice Sentences

He did *what*?!

This is *it*!

T Near the Letter N

T often becomes a glottal stop when it appears near the nasal consonant N. Because of this, the T is bypassed and the consonant N is pronounced. It may feel as if the consonant T has disappeared.

Finding the Glottal T with N

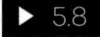

1. Bring your tongue tip up to the gum ridge as if making a consonant T.
2. As you do this, stop the airflow momentarily to create a glottal stop.
3. Keep your tongue tip on the gum ridge as you push air through the nose, in effect switching the sound to an N.
4. It may feel as though the sound 'pops' through your nose to make this action.

Then repeat this exercise speaking words aloud, starting with the word 'button'.

Practice Sentences

The button on the mitten is hidden.

Martin is writing sentences about mountains.

I'm giving you an important letter to deliver to Mr Barton.

The Word 'To'

It is often the smallest words in any accent that can catch actors out. This is because function words – the words that help with the grammatical sense and structure of phrase – are often shortened. One of these important function words is the word 'to'.

In American English the word 'to' changes when in an unstressed syllable:

1. The T becomes almost like a D. This is the 'flap T', which may feel like a flutter in the mouth.
2. The vowel becomes shortened into an unstressed short vowel, called a schwa /ə/. This vowel sounds like a very short UH sound, with the tongue resting in the middle of the mouth and the lips relaxed.

Take note of this change in action on the word 'to' because it can help you sound more like a native speaker.

Practice Sentences

What do I need to do for you tomorrow?

I'm going to the store.

All I want you to do is to love me.

Helpful Hint: Sometimes a native speaker will pronounce the consonant T in 'to' the same way as any other initial T. This is also correct and can be used for clarity and at times when precision is needed. However, be sure that the overall delivery does not become too percussive, with an overemphasis on the consonant T. The General American accent tends to place its energy in the vowels, not the consonants!

Text Practice

Below each text there are guidelines on which pronunciation choice to use depending on how T appears in the word and in the sentence.

Erik from The Humans by Stephen Karam

❝...yeah, well what I think's funny is how you guys, you move to big cities and trash Scranton, when Momo almost killed herself getting outta New York – she didn't have a real toilet in this city, and now her granddaughter moves right back to the place she struggled to escape...

- *T in the middle of a word*: ci<u>t</u>ies, ge<u>tt</u>ing, ou<u>tt</u>a, granddaugh<u>t</u>er
- *T at the end of a word becomes D or a glottal*: wha<u>t I</u> think, toile<u>t in</u>
- *T at the end of a word becomes a glottal*: righ<u>t </u>back
- *T near letter N*: Scra<u>nt</u>on
- *The word 'to'*: the consonant T can be pronounced as usual, or it can reduce to a 'flap T', which feels like a very quick D.

Becca from Rabbit Hole by David Lindsay-Abaire

❝Do you really not know me, Howie? Do you really not know how utterly impossible that would be? To erase him? No matter how many things I give to charity, or how many art projects I box up, do you really think I don't see him every second of every day? And okay, I'm trying to make things a little easier on myself by hiding some of the photos, and giving away the clothes, but that does not mean I'm trying to erase him. That tape was an accident. And believe me, I will beat myself up about it forever, I'm sure. Like everything else that I could've prevented but didn't.

- *T in the middle of a word*: u<u>tt</u>erly, ma<u>tt</u>er, chari<u>ty</u>, li<u>ttl</u>e, pho<u>t</u>os
- *T at the end of a word becomes a D or glottal*: abou<u>t it</u>, tha<u>t I</u>
- *T at the end of a word becomes a glottal*: no<u>t</u> know, tha<u>t</u> would, ar<u>t</u> projects, don<u>'t</u> see, tha<u>t</u> does, no<u>t</u> mean, tha<u>t</u> tape, acciden<u>t</u>, bea<u>t</u> myself, didn<u>'t</u>
- *T near letter N*: preven<u>t</u>ed

After practising the individual T words, go back and read the speech again to increase your skills in practice.

Vowel /æ/ as in TR<u>A</u>P and B<u>A</u>TH

The vowel /æ/ as in TR<u>A</u>P is distinct in the General American accent and is a key vowel to practise. In fact, the TR<u>A</u>P vowel is used in many words when other speakers of English do not: words like LAST, ASK and PASS.

I like the phonetic symbol that represents the sound because it's simply a + e pushed together. However, the TR<u>A</u>P vowel is not a diphthong. A diphthong is a vowel created by the mouth moving between two different vowel sounds – but the mouth does not move between two vowels to make the TR<u>A</u>P vowel.

Instead, the vowel is almost like a blend. It's as if the voice hovers between both /a/ and /e/ to create its own distinct vowel. So, while the vowel is not a diphthong, it may feel like it has similar properties, which is why this combined /æ/ letter does a good job of symbolising the sound.

Finding the Vowel

To find the TRAP /æ/ vowel:

1. Your mouth is open, with your tongue tip resting behind your bottom teeth.
2. The front of your tongue slightly arches forward, which may feel as if the tongue is trying to escape your mouth.
3. It may feel as if a small coin is resting on the front of your tongue.
4. Your tongue does not move or glide from its position as the vowel is sounded with the voice.
5. It may feel as if there is vibration towards the front of your face as you make this sound.

apple   sabotage   challenge   radical   cat

Practice Sentences

Mac will be in the shadows holding a hat at the top of Act Two.

Half of all cats have their vaccinations against rat bacteria.

The fact is that sapphire does not flatter me at all.

Additional TRAP /æ/ Words

There are some words where American speakers use the TRAP vowel which may differ from other accents of English. Notably, the American accent overwhelmingly uses the TRAP vowel when 'A' comes before S, F, TH and N:

a + s	pass, glass, master, ask
a + f	calf, photograph
a + th	rather, bath, path
a + n	plant, dance, can't, answer

Practice Sentences

Patsy took her last photograph of the castle while standing on the grass.

Staff have a hard time controlling the questions asked by the class.

I would rather take a bath than complete a task.

The Nasalised AN, AM & ANG

The TRAP vowel becomes nasalised when followed by a nasal vowel sound: N, M, NG. Nasalised means that the airflow escapes through your nose instead of through your mouth. This happens by lowering the soft palate in the back of your mouth. As you keep the soft palate low, the sound is amplified through your nose creating this distinct nasal sound.

You will feel extra vibration in the nose when voicing this sound. You can check if the sound is nasalised by placing a finger under your nose and sensing airflow exiting your nostrils as you make the sound. You can visualise that the sound is exploding out of the bridge of your nose and your cheekbones in order to place the voice up in the nose.

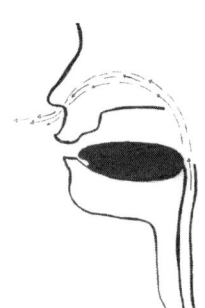

To find the nasal AN / AM / ANG:

1. Bring your tongue into the TRAP /æ/ position as demonstrated previously.
2. Allow yourself to sense your soft palate releasing and resting low in the back of your mouth.
3. When voiced, the TRAP vowel should feel like it's coming up and out of your nose.

4. You can feel vibration in the nose, or on the bridge of the nose and the cheeks, as you make this sound.
5. The vowel is short, and the tongue does not move from its position as the vowel is voiced.

▶ 6.3

a + n	answer, plant, dance, January
a + m	tamper, camera, Sam, hammer
a + ng	sang, rang, mangled, languish

Playing with the Nasal Sound

The nasal TR<u>A</u>P vowel is very similar to French nasal vowels. Experiment by putting on your most over-the-top French accent in order to find this specific vowel in the General American accent.

▶ 6.4

1. Start by voicing an over-the-top 'French' stereotype sound: 'Hon hon hon!'
2. You might also imagine honking geese or a honking horn in order to move vibration up to your nose: 'Honk! Honk!'
3. Now change the vowel /æ/ as in TR<u>A</u>P, but continue sensing vibration up in your nose.
4. Your soft palate will need to stay released and resting low for your voice to travel up into the back of your nose.

Practice Sentences ▶ 6.5

Nancy can't stand transporting plants in the trunk of her car.

Dan and I had the chance to dance the night away at my aunt's party.

The archaeologist took a sample from the land next to the Amazon.

Text Practice

Diwata from Speech & Debate *by Stephen Karam*

❝Welcome to the first pod<u>cast</u> entry of my diary, updated daily at monoblog.com. Let's hear it for my b<u>an</u>d – that's <u>Ca</u>sio in the background. <u>Ca</u>sio's been progr<u>amm</u>ed to play the only three chords I know over and over while I improvise a new song, live, before your ears, America. Ideally, the music would be a little more interesting, but I <u>can't</u> play and sing at the same time, <u>an</u>d I have no friends to help me out. 'But Diwata,' you're saying to yourselves, 'You're so odd and frumpy – you must h<u>a</u>ve friends.' But no, I don't. All I h<u>a</u>ve is my music.

- *TRAP /æ/ vowel words*: podcast, Casio, have
- *Nasalised words*: programmed, can't, and

After practising each word, go back and read the monologue again to increase your skills in practice.

Vowel /ɑ/ as in SP<u>A</u>, L<u>O</u>T and TH<u>OU</u>GHT

The vowel /ɑ/ as in SP<u>A</u> manages to cover a lot of ground in the General American accent. In fact, it can be used in a wide range of words and spellings such as those in the table below:

SP<u>A</u>	father, calm, palm, lava
L<u>O</u>T	god, vodka, John, positive
CL<u>O</u>TH	off, loss, soft, gone
TH<u>OU</u>GHT	bought, fought, sought
<u>AU</u>GUST	caught, daughter, Australia, autumn
L<u>AW</u>	hawk, yawn, awful, jaw
<u>ALL</u>	fall, walk, small, halt

Before continuing, it's important to acknowledge that there are many different accepted American pronunciations of the words listed above. Speakers may differentiate these vowels depending on the region they originate from. If you are undertaking a role that requires specific regionalisms, it's important to make adjustments as necessary.

However, for the sake of ease and clarity, all of these words *can* be pronounced with the same vowel in an American accent. It is for this reason I am encouraging you to use the same vowel on all of the words listed above.

A quick note that this is yet another instance where the English language pronounces vowels differently from how they are written. This becomes more and more apparent as you develop your experience working with accents, but you should keep it in mind as you practise.

Finding the Vowel

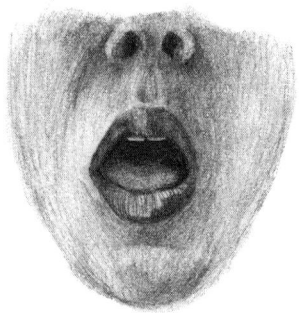

1. Your mouth is fully open, with your tongue tip resting behind your bottom teeth.
2. The body of your tongue is resting low in your mouth.

3. Allow yourself to feel as if you are cupping a small coin as it sits on the back of your tongue. You can also pretend as if a doctor has asked you to open your mouth and say 'Ahh'.
4. Most importantly, there is very little lip-rounding required to make this sound. Your lips should be sitting neutral, neither spread nor rounded too far forward.

Practice Sentences

Tom is talking to Paul about his daughter's law school.

I bought a cup of coffee while walking my dog.

The restaurant boss didn't like that the water came at no cost to the throngs of customers.

The jolly toddler knocked over the tower of blocks and balls.

It's best to be honest about the knowledge you have and not get caught in a naughty lie!

Flexibility and Precision

It is useful to practise moving between the vowel /ɑ/ as in SP<u>A</u> and the sound OR /ɔɚ/ as in F<u>OR</u>CE explored in the consonant R chapter. This is because these sounds are distinctly different in the American accent, and it can be a tongue-twister for other speakers of English.

As a reminder:

1. In words with the OR /ɔɚ/ as in F<u>OR</u>CE vowel, your lips round forward and your tongue engages to pronounce the consonant R. It may feel like you are

'kissing' the word as you speak it. The consonant R will feel fused to the vowel.

2. In words with the /ɑ/ as in SP<u>A</u> vowel, your mouth opens and your tongue is low in the mouth. It may feel as if you are cupping a small coin on the back of your tongue.
3. Allow your lips and tongue to be flexible enough to move between both sounds.

Practice Sentences

> The court of law in North Australia awarded John four hundred dollars.
>
> We all saw that our father was sore after his fall in Cornwall.
>
> George bought a new door to transform the awful cottage into an adorable home.

Troubleshooting

Keep your mouth open and your tongue resting low and back in the mouth to make this vowel correctly. Additionally, your lips should be open and neither rounding too far forward nor spreading too wide.

However, if you run into trouble, here are some tips that can help depending on the following circumstances:

The lips are rounding forward too much

If the lips round forward too much, you can end up pronouncing a different vowel entirely. Often, this is when an American accent starts creeping towards the other side of the Atlantic and begins to sound a little British. In this case you want to train the mouth to open and widen in this sound. Lightly rest your hands on either side of your face as you practise the individual words. Allow yourself to visualise the mouth and lips opening and releasing. You can use your hands to guide the muscles resting underneath. Then release your hands and repeat your practice, keeping the same sensation you felt with your hands on your face.

The mouth is moving between two vowels

Sometimes actors will accidentally move their mouth between two vowels when practising this sound, particularly on words like th<u>ou</u>ght, c<u>au</u>ght and l<u>aw</u>. This will create a diphthong, and the accent may start to sound like a stereotypical New York City accent.

However, the mouth stays resting in one position for this vowel in the General American accent. Lightly rest a finger on your lips you practise the individual words and practice sentences. Allow yourself to visualise the mouth opening and widening. Feel your lips open and keeping still through the vowel. Then release your finger and repeat your practice, keeping the same sensation you felt with your finger resting on your lips. Using a mirror can help in this practice, as you will be able to better see the mouth in action.

The tongue is too far forward and the lips are spreading wide

You will also end up pronouncing a different vowel if your tongue is sitting too far forward in the mouth. The lips might start to spread too wide as well. This mouth position veers the American accent into caricature. In this case, you need to train the body of your tongue to rest at the back of your mouth while pronouncing the vowel. Your lips can release forward as well.

Imagine that you are cupping a small coin on the back of your tongue. Keeping this imaginary coin in place, speak through the practice words and phrases slowly. You may choose to keep the image of the coin in mind throughout your practice, releasing the image once you feel you have mastered the sound.

Text Practice

Richard from Teenage Dick *by Mike Lew*

❝Now that the winter formal gives way to glorious spring fling we find our r<u>o</u>cks-for-brains hero Eddie – the quarterback – sleeping through his j<u>o</u>b as junior class president. 'Oh? Was I president? I've had so many *concussions* I must've forg<u>o</u>t!' Yeah. He's Phoebus Ap<u>o</u>llo whereas I am but feeble. He makes sport of governance whereas I am <u>not</u> one who is shaped for sports.

I, Richard, am junior class *secretary*. Third in line behind Eddie the quarter-brains and Clarissa the goodie-goodie vice-president. *Welllll*. Maybe I can't play foot<u>ball</u>, but I can run a play. The senior elections are upon us and from here I will v<u>au</u>lt past my inglorious station. <u>Not</u> by a pity vote. <u>Not</u> by campaigning. But by systematically destroying the c<u>om</u>petition. I'll take down Clarissa AND Eddie AND hold dominion over <u>all</u> of this school.

Note: This text includes examples of the vowel AH /ɑ/ as in SP<u>A</u> and the sound OR /ɔɚ/ as in F<u>OR</u>CE to help you practise moving between both sounds.

Vowel /oʊ/ as in G<u>OA</u>T

The vowel /oʊ/ as in G<u>OA</u>T is a diphthong created by the mouth moving between two different vowel sounds. Because of this specific action, the /oʊ/ as in G<u>OA</u>T diphthong is a key vowel to practise so that you can perfect the sound for performance.

know   don't   r<u>o</u>se   R<u>o</u>me
<u>o</u>cean   sl<u>o</u>wly

Finding the Vowel

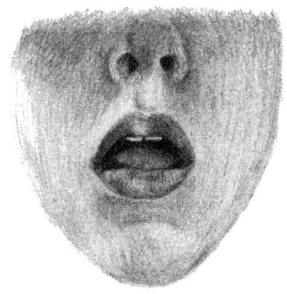

To find the /oʊ/ as in GOAT vowel:

1. The mouth starts with your lips slightly parted and the body of your tongue sitting towards the back of your mouth.
2. The vowel finishes with your lips more rounded and the body of your tongue slightly more forward from the starting position. The ending vowel sound is the vowel /ʊ/ as in FOOT.
3. The mouth glides from the first position to the second position as the vowel is pronounced. This glide action helps to distinguish this vowel as a diphthong and is a feature of the American accent.
4. It may feel as if this vowel lives very far back in the mouth. I encourage you to imagine a small coin resting on the back of your tongue to gently bring the tongue into position.

Practice Sentences

Row row row your boat…

Soak the noble's robe in soap and rose water.

Joan's family is nobility from Rome, and she isn't below acting holier than we know her to be.

She wrapped her toes in ropes before floating out in the ocean in a boat.

/oʊ/ as in GOAL

When /oʊ/ as in GOAT is followed by an L, the vowel can feel very rounded and almost swallowed. Be sure to practise differentiating between /ɑ/ as in SP<u>A</u> and /oʊ/ as in G<u>OA</u>L – when the vowels appear before an L.

Paul — pole

ball — bold

call — cold

mall — mould

doll — dole

fall — fold

hall — whole

Saul — soul

Practice Sentences

The old man told me he has a cold.

Don't forget to go slowly when you fold the clothes.

Paul says to call Cole before buying that pole at the mall.

Text Practice

Elias from John *by Annie Baker*

❝ Well. S<u>o</u>. We met in a parking lot and Spooky took us through a graveyard and then down this alleyway where like they used to dump a lot of dead <u>so</u>ldier bodies or something and we had these like beeper sticks that would go off if they sensed like 'gh*o*st energy' or whatever and it was starting to feel pretty lame but then she took us to the Farnsworth House?...

And then she just let us like r*oa*m around on our *o*wn and take pictures. And anyway. I went upstairs and into this like antiquey like kid's bedroom? Like apparently a kid lived there in the nineteenth century and they kept all his stuff or something. And anyway I just took a picture of the room because it was kind of cool to see a nineteenth century like little kid's bed but THEN after I left I looked at the ph*oto* and...

- /oʊ/ *as in GOAT*: so, ghost, roam, own, photo
- /oʊ/ *as in GOAL*: soldier

The Details

There is a well-known saying: 'the devil is in the details'. This idiom means that something that may seem simple at first can take time to master – and that it's the small details which make the difference between success and failure. This is certainly true for accent work where it's often the details that can make or break an accent. For example, short or small words can be important for the very fact that they seem so unimportant. These details require precision, but the reward is great. Once the details are perfected, you are well on your way to centring the accent in your own voice.

I've included some of these 'detail' rules below. It would be difficult to cover everything in one book, but these are the important details I see come up time and time again.

/ʌ/ as in CUP

For some actors, the vowel UH /ʌ/ as in CUP in the American accent will be different than their own pronunciation of the word. This may include people from Northern England, the Midlands, Ireland and Wales. Multilingual actors might also want to work on this sound because this vowel sound is not found in many major world languages.

Finding the Vowel

1. Rest the tongue tip just behind your bottom front teeth.
2. The body of your tongue sits towards the back of your mouth, and the middle of your tongue rises slightly. It may feel as if a small coin is resting on the back of your tongue.
3. Your lips are not rounded when voicing this vowel.

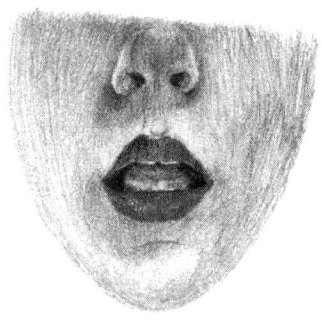

Take care when practising, as there are a number of spellings that may be pronounced with the vowel UH /ʌ/ as in C<u>U</u>P.

u	cut, much, lung, run
o	done, mother, love, onion
ou	touch, enough, Southern
oo	blood, flood

In an American accent, the vowel UH /ʌ/ as in CUP is the same vowel used in the word WHAT. This is different from other many other accents of English and is a unique feature of the American accent. In fact, you can memorise these five words containing the vowel because they come up time and time again:

▶ 9.2

what   was   of   because   from

A tip for remembering the pronunciation of these words is to imagine how Americans often write these words online or in text messaging. In this case, I like the 'faux-netics' spellings borrowed from internet-speak:

Word	Internet Spelling
what	wut / wt
was	wuz / wz
of	uv
because	becuz
from	frum / frm

Practice Sentences

It's always funny when my brother and cousin get together for supper. This is because I'm from a large Southern family and all of us love playing jokes on one another. We even get the puppy involved sometimes! However, my mother is a fuddy duddy and doesn't like it so much. One time she even called a judge to get us to stop doing dumb stuff. She said we were wreaking havoc on vulnerable adults. I can't even remember what the call was for, but it made for a lovely story at the time.

TH

TH is pronounced with the tongue tip almost touching the back of the teeth or with the tongue slightly between the teeth. TH is a *fricative* sound, meaning airflow creates friction in order to make the consonant. If you recall, there are two TH sounds – one is made with the breath and the other is made with vibration. The breath TH appears in words like THINK, THIN and MONTH. The voiced TH will feel like vibration on the back of your teeth and appears in words like THEM, THESE and MOTHER. Differentiate this sound from the consonants F and V, which are made when the bottom lip touches the top teeth.

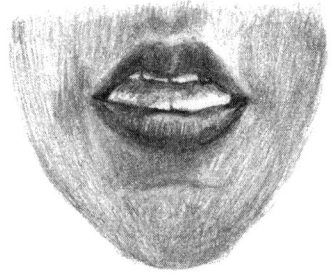

Mouth Warm-up

Practise moving between these two exercises as a warm-up and test for your mouth:

Unvoiced TH (all breath):   TH – F – S – F – TH
Voiced TH (all vibration):   TH – V – Z – V – TH

Practice Sentences

> Every Thursday, brothers Frank and Keith go together to visit the resting place of their mother Edith. But in actual fact, this year is the first time they can stand to be together! They fought for three years after their mother's death. Keith thought that Frank was a thief, so he froze access to thousands of dollars in Edith's accounts. Frank had no faith that he could change his brother's mind to think otherwise. This forced Frank to go to their father Seth for help. Seth told Frank to set up a meeting on the heath for them both to meet. Thank goodness he did, because once the brothers talked through their grievances they were able to put this filthy fight behind them.

/u/ as in GOOSE

Take notice when the vowel /u/ as in GOOSE appears after a gum-ridge consonant. A gum-ridge consonant is a consonant made by the tip of the tongue on the gum ridge behind the top front teeth. The gum ridge consonants are T, D, N, L, S and Z.

In an American accent, speakers move the tongue directly into the vowel without adding a linking sound between the consonant and vowel. In this case:

tune → toon	new → noo

Practise by moving through different vowels before landing on the /u/ as in G<u>OO</u>SE vowel. Keep your tongue bouncing lightly off the gum ridge and directly to the vowel.

▶ 9.6

1	2	3
tea	dee	knee
ta	da	na
toe	dough	no
too	do	new

Practice Sentences

It's such a nuisance to find tuna in New York. Every Tuesday I grab some aluminum and go out to the sand dunes to look for fish. I assume I'll find something but it's always bad news. Then I catch the train due at two o'clock to get back into town. During the ride I sing a tune to myself. It's a consuming pursuit.

Note: This does not happen in other words like <u>beau</u>tiful and <u>mu</u>sic. In these words /u/ as in G<u>OO</u>SE is not after a gum-ridge consonant.

Words That Shorten in Connected Speech

There are a few words that have a tendency to shorten in connected speech. This process is called *reduction* and involves replacing a vowel with an unstressed short vowel, called a schwa /ə/. Using the schwa can help an actor sound more like a native speaker and can also make the accent easier to pronounce at speed.

Word	Quick Speech Version	Example
for	fer /fɚ/	Who's this for? It's for him.
your	yer /jɚ/	Where's your car?
or	er /ɚ/	Do you want chicken or beef?
are	er /ɚ/	Where are you going?
can	kn /kən/	Can you get that for me?
sure	sher /ʃɚ/	Sure thing!
our	ar /ɑɚ/	This is our house.
to	tuh /tə/	I'm going to the store.
and	n /ən/	Peanut butter and jelly.

Practice Sentences ▶ 9.9

If you want to order a pizza, you first need to talk to your brothers and sisters. Ask if they want pepperoni or sausage. Then figure out how much your father is willing to pay. When the driver comes to our house, be sure to give him a nice tip. When are you going to call?

Been

Nearly everywhere in the United States (with a few exceptions) the word 'been' is pronounced 'bin'. This word can take some time to practise, I suspect because it is a small word but spoken aloud often. However, it is another small detail that will bring a layer of believability and elevate your accent work.

Practice Sentences ▶ 9.10

The kids have <u>been</u> to the gym in the city.

Where have you <u>been</u>?

Syllable Stress

There are many words pronounced nearly identically between British and American English, but the stressed syllable might differ. I've outlined a few key rules below with some practice sentences.

Do not worry about remembering all of the rules at once. Through practice it will become more and more apparent to you where the syllables change. Speak the following exercises aloud to consolidate the changes in your voice and body.

First Syllable Stressed	Second Syllable Stressed
<u>frus</u>trate	mass<u>age</u>
<u>cre</u>mate	barr<u>age</u>
<u>do</u>nate	ball<u>et</u>
<u>va</u>cate	rec<u>luse</u>
<u>con</u>troversy	de<u>bris</u>
<u>prin</u>cess	a<u>dult</u>
<u>tra</u>chea	Thanks<u>giving</u>

Practice Sentences

The princess is frustrated about the controversy surrounding her love to donate.

After Thanksgiving, the adult recluse went to the ballet and got a massage.

Words Ending in -erry / -ary / -ory

Fully pronounce the vowels in words ending with -erry, -ary and -ory. I have underlined the <u>first syllable stress</u>, and *italicised* the second syllable in the words below.

▶ 9.12

<u>blue</u>*berry*
<u>straw</u>*berry*

<u>rose</u>*mary*
<u>mil</u>*itary*
<u>li</u>*brary*

<u>ter</u>*ritory*
<u>ca</u>*tegory*

Practice Sentence

Rosemary's territory is near the military's supply of strawberries.

Finally...

There are many words that differ between British English and American English. This may be a change in pronunciation of the word, a change in syllable stress, a change in how a word is written, or even a change in definition and meaning. It would be nearly impossible to memorise the American pronunciation of every word that could one day come up in a text.

I encourage you to use an online dictionary with pronunciation audio files for both British and American English when you come across a word and you are unsure of its pronunciation. In that case you can listen to the American pronunciation and adjust accordingly. Equally, you can create a list of words that come up often as a tool to remind yourself. And be very careful regarding culture-specific terminology: proper nouns such as the names of national parks or past presidents can have specific pronunciations that can give away a non-native speaker!

Practice Sentences

Here is a text with a few common words that come up time and time again:

Yesterday, Craig and I left the territory looking for something to eat. We passed a few depots before finally finding a shopping centre full of food. It seemed like everyone who is anyone was there. I was going to get the risotto until I saw how many herbs they had put in it! Craig decided on a blueberry yogurt. He's very particular about getting all of his daily vitamins. However, procuring the yogurt involved standing in line next to the compost bin, which was not ideal. We waited about twenty minutes before deciding that the whole process was taking too long. We were worried that someone might ask us where we had been, so we figured that we might as well get back to town. The rest is history.

3. The Music

A voice colleague of mine once said that an actor who has mastered the music of an accent can fool ninety per cent of their audience. Although that claim has not been proven, it does serve to introduce an important piece of accent performance. The music of an accent consists of a range of elements including the *rhythm, stress, melody, pitch, volume, pace, vocal quality* and *intonation patterns*.

Up until this point we have spent a lot of time on the vowels and consonants of the General American accent. The vowels and consonants will help you achieve the basics of an accent. However, it is the music of an accent that is usually perceived by the audience.

This is because as humans we listen and hear other peoples' voices on a wider, more macro-level. We first perceive the overall music of a speaker's voice and speech. It's only with closer listening that we then pick up specific individual vowels and consonants. In fact, music is the first part of language that we are exposed to in utero. Due to this primal connection it makes sense that it plays such an integral role in accent work.

Listen

The most basic step to learning the music of an accent is simple: listen to native speakers. You can find a handful of voices in the recordings below:

▶ 10.1: Story 1

▶ 10.2: Story 2

▶ 10.3: Story 3

▶ 10.4: Story 4

▶ 10.5: Story 5

▶ 10.6: Story 6

▶ 10.7: Story 7

General Rules

The first question to arise for you might be: 'Great – what are the music rules for a General American accent?' My response to that question is that mastering the music of an accent is a bit like learning to play jazz. You can learn the fundamentals, but a master should also be able to improvise around the notes. No two speakers sound the same, so there are *many right ways* to interpret a line in an American accent. Once an actor understands the broad strokes of the music of an American accent, the actor can then connect that framework to fit the character, their intentions, text and subtext. That is when an actor can truly 'riff' in the accent.

Here are a few guidelines regarding the music of a General American accent to get you started:

- The overall energy may feel like it's moving through the vowels of the words. This can be heard when speakers lengthen the vowels in stressed words.
- Rhythm is tied to emphasis. Place weight and length on the operative words to create emphasis.
- Feel the voice vibrating in your body, as opposed to placing the sound outside of your body. You may feel vibration off the back of your mouth and also in your face and head.
- Pitch range can be narrowed compared to accents of England, Scotland, Wales and Ireland. It can feel as if you are using about four or five notes in your range.
- Americans can give the impression of thinking and speaking at the same time. This may be cultural, but it can affect the music of the accent.
- However, it is important to not become overly seduced by the music. You will want to play the scene so as to not drown out the sense and meaning in sing-songy repetition.

Embodying the Music of an Accent

I encourage you to bring all of this work off the page and into your body by moving. The voice is made by the structures of the body, so how we speak affects our whole person – reflecting not only where we come from, but also our personalities and what we want to say. Physical activities such as walking or moving will help bring the American accent out of your head and into an embodied place.

Approach the following exercises through *layering*. Focus on one exercise at a time. After the exercise is completed, let go of the element explored, but trust that your body and voice will retain the experience.

Linguists speak of the music (also known as 'prosody') of an accent in parts: the rhythm, stress, melody, pitch, volume, pace, vocal quality and intonation. So when I say music in this chapter, I am referring to the relationship between all of these parts. However, I'm not sure it's useful to teach the parts in isolation for acting. That would be like asking a musician to only play one component of a concerto. All of these components form part of the whole accent and are best practised together for a fully realised accent in performance.

Learning an Accent by Ear

Some actors enjoy learning an accent by ear, and find they pick up accents easily this way. Learning an accent by ear can be a great way to access the first broad brushstrokes of the accent. This practice can be enhanced through Conscious Listening and Conscious Voicing, using audio clips of a sample speaker.

As discussed earlier, Conscious Listening comes into play because *you cannot reproduce a sound that you cannot hear*. Through Conscious Listening you will begin to hear and understand the music of the accent.

Conscious Voicing might also be described as mimicking or copying the sounds aloud with a heightened awareness of the task. Voicing the music of the accent in a concentrated way will begin to move the accent into your voice and body.

Some actors find that immersing themselves in the American accent is enough to master the music of the accent for performance. In that case, consistently listening to interviews, podcasts, radio or video of native speakers may be enough to get the accent into the ear and voice. But other actors may want a more systematic approach, as outlined next.

Beginning Stages

When you first begin listening to American speakers, start to notice their accent compared to your own voice.

1. Is the *pitch range* wide or monotone?
2. Is the *pace* fast or slow?
3. Is the voice *louder or softer* on certain words?
4. Are the *vowels* stretched long or shortened and quick?

This will vary between speakers, but it is useful to have a sense of where you are starting from in order to understand what changes to make. Take time to listen to a range of American speakers, either through podcasts or from film and television.

Working with Sample Speaker Audio

I suggest that you pick a native sample speaker of the General American accent. This can be someone whose voice fits the character, or a native speaker whose voice fits the actor. Although a General American accent is easily identifiable, the music of the accent can change depending on the type of person: old or young, male or female, and from various ethnic backgrounds. It is for this reason that native sample speaker audio can help you get specific.

You can source audio from online interviews, podcasts, social media apps, or even recording a native speaker on your phone. Using the audio from a sample speaker, I suggest first taking a small clip of the conversation running about fifteen seconds. Then listen to even shorter sections of this clip of five seconds or less. You can also use an audio-editing software if you prefer separate clips to work from.

Play the first five-second section a few times through to begin to hear the melody, rhythm, stress and intonation patterns. Then begin Conscious Voicing, mimicking the clip and repeating the cycle through at least five times. I encourage you to record yourself and listen back each time to compare your take to the sample speaker. Apply this targeted vocal repetition to the other shortened sections of the fifteen-second clip.

Once finished, speak the entire fifteen-second clip aloud in your own voice, minding the rhythm, melody, stress and intonation patterns heard in the original clip. Through this work, you will have begun the process of feeling the accent in your own voice and body. You can always return to this fifteen-second clip to ground yourself again in the accent.

Catchphrases

Using a few 'catchphrases' from a range of General American speakers can be an excellent way to connect the accent to your voice and then on to text. A catchphrase can be any short phrase that helps to launch you into the accent. When listening to a sample speaker, write down three phrases that feel representative of the accent. These might be phrases that stick out to you on an initial listen, or something the speaker said that you can easily remember. Memorise these catchphrases just as the speaker spoke them – both in terms of pronunciation and the musicality of their speech.

Helpful Hint: These catchphrases can be very short. In fact, the shorter the better. Aim for one short thought per catchphrase.

I have isolated a few phrases from both male and female General American speakers.

10.8

Female Sample Speaker:

1. Look at this and remember what this looks like.
2. And then I moved to New York City when I was fourteen.
3. It took me, like an hour to get to school.

Male Sample Speaker:

1. Basically, she was working for the Shakespeare Globe Theatre.
2. My mom happened to be in town visiting.
3. And she shows up at the top of the stairs…

Catchphrases with Text

Once you feel comfortable with your catchphrases, you can then begin to alternate the catchphrases with your text. Speak your catchphrase aloud, followed by a bit of your performance text. Repeat the process, slowly working through your text while returning to your catchphrases. It may be useful to think of weaving back and forth between catchphrases and bits of text.

The catchphrase will ground you in the accent, while the text will encourage you to play with the foundation established by the catchphrase. As you start, your focus should be on experimenting and playing with sound, instead of getting the text 'right' immediately.

Zack from Belleville *by Amy Herzog*

[*Catchphrase*] **Basically, she was working for the Shakespeare Globe Theatre.**

[*Text*] She's trying to go off her medication.

My mom happened to be in town visiting.

Not trying, she's going off.

And she shows up at the top of the stairs.

It's torture.

Basically, she was working for the Shakespeare Globe Theatre.

But I'm not allowed to say anything, because that would be *unsupportive*.

My mom happened to be in town visiting.

And this is a *period of transition*.

And she shows up at the top of the stairs.

Helpful Hint: You may want to run through this exercise multiple times. Each time through, you can slowly reduce the number of times you speak your catchphrases until you are only speaking the text.

Draw the Accent

As a continuation of the catchphrase exercise, some visual learners may appreciate this next one. Using your catchphrases, you can draw the accent's musical journey to give yourself a visual representation of the American accent.

▶ 10.8

1. Look at this and remember what this looks like.

2. And then I moved to New York City when I was fourteen.

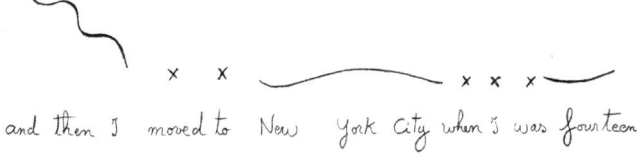

3. It took me, like an hour to get to school.

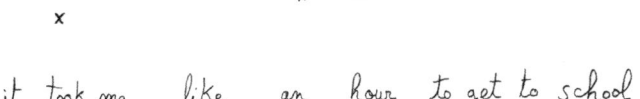

You can then draw the catchphrase patterns directly onto the text to help guide your eye and your voice whilst practising the accent. Feel free to try out a number of visual patterns as you go along.

Working with Operative Words

Operative words are the words in a phrase that convey the meaning. Operative words are usually nouns, verbs, and sometimes adjectives and adverbs. Think of operative words like the words you would use when writing a telegram. They are the words that are absolutely necessary for getting the information across to your listener.

Finding the operative words of your text helps to connect with the overall music and flow of the text. It also forces the actor to play the story for its meaning and avoid becoming 'stuck' in the confines of the accent.

Kendra from Gloria by Branden Jacobs-Jenkins

❝A very bad thing happened to both of us! – to all of us! – yet you seem to think it happened only to you.

Telegram words: THING BOTH. ALL. YOU THINK ONLY YOU.

Mark up your text for the operative words. Then speak the operative words aloud once through. It may sound like you're reading your text in telegram format.

Then speak your text in full, taking care that the operative words act as your guide to the rhythm of the accent.

Kendra from Gloria by Branden Jacobs-Jenkins

❝A very bad thing happened to <u>both</u> of us! – to <u>all</u> of us! – yet you seem to think it happened <u>only</u> to <u>you</u>. <u>Why</u> is that? Because you went to <u>Gloria's</u> dumb <u>party</u> and she <u>saved</u> you? Because you were 'a <u>witness</u>' to everyone's last <u>moments</u>? Because you're

<u>entitled</u> enough to think the world automatically <u>cares</u> about you and what you <u>feel</u> and what you <u>saw</u>? And <u>why</u> is that? You did <u>not</u> survive some <u>holocaust</u>.

Helpful Hint: If you feel you are stressing too many words, try to identify the single most important operative word per phrase. Repeat the exercise above.

Working with Character

The music of any voice and accent is influenced by a number of factors beyond the basic rules. Just as your voice is not monotone or a repetition of the same pattern, neither is your character's voice.

The text itself is a good place to begin, because a playwright writes with the character's voice in mind. The character's rhythms, attitudes and point of view inform not only what they say, but how they say it. Notice the character's vocabulary and grammar choices. Moreover, connect with the situation your character is currently in, and the other people your character is speaking with. A calm dialogue with friends will be different than a heated argument, and a presentation or sermon will be different than a private conversation. Linking the accent to your character's intention and subtext will create a more believable sound.

Exercises Exploring Music Linked to Text

It is natural to be uncertain when transitioning from more technical aspects of accent-learning to using the accent freely with your text. After all, it may be the first time you aren't copying anyone. Instead, you are now centring the accent and text in your own voice. You may never hear everything your character says spoken aloud by a native speaker – and that's okay. There are many *right* ways to interpret the text in the target accent. Trust that the accent work you have done separate from the text will help to support your work when you are speaking the text.

I encourage you to really play with the text in the following exercises. Moving the accent into the voice and body will bring you beyond mimicry. With dedicated practice you will come to see that performing in an accent is both an art and a skill.

Using Drumming, Clapping or Tapping

Speak your text aloud in the accent while physically drumming the beat of the accent. I enjoy using a real drum, but you can easily use your hands clapping together or one hand tapping on a surface to feel the rhythm and stress of the accent on your text. The most important part is to drum or tap *at the same time you speak aloud*. I often see actors unintentionally drumming or clapping after they've already spoken the target word aloud. Bring these two actions in tandem to feel the full effects of this exercise.

1. *Tap the Stressed Syllables*: Speak your text aloud once through while drumming or tapping out the stressed syllables as they appear in each word. Make a note of any words whose stressed syllable changes from your own accent.

2. *Tap the Stressed Words*: Speak your text aloud again from the beginning, but this time drum or tap on the operative words, those you feel are the most important to get the story or your point across.

3. *Tap the Final Word*: Finally, speak your text aloud from the beginning and drum or tap on the final word of each thought. As there is a drive towards the end of the phrase in the American accent, tapping the final word

can help establish this press to the finish. Of course, not every final word will be stressed when you're performing as you would sound repetitive, but this exercise can give a sense of that drive to your accent preparation.

Using a Ball

Speak your text aloud in the accent while throwing a ball. You can throw the ball to a partner or throw the ball against a wall. Release the ball to your partner or to the wall at the end of each thought. Allow yourself to feel the drive towards the end of the phrase found in the American accent. As you continue this exercise, stay connected with your free and released breath. Breathe in as you catch the ball, and then use your breath to power the voice and thought on the release of the ball.

Using Movement and Dance

As stated at the beginning of the chapter, I encourage you to get up off your chair and begin to move when approaching the music of an accent. Moving will help free the accent from the head and allow it to nestle into a rooted place in the body, breath and voice.

Moving with an Audio Sample

Listening to your sample speaker audio, begin to move around the room with the music of their voice. Allow yourself to sense their rhythm, stress and melody patterns in your own body. Notice if your centre of gravity has changed. Take note of their pacing and pitch changes as well. Once you sense their accent in your body, you are welcome to jot down a few notes on what feels important.

Moving Using Text

You can also transition this movement work to text. Deeply connect with your character's centre of gravity. You may even have a sense of where they breathe; perhaps in the back, the belly or the chest. Begin walking around the room with the new connection. Speak the text aloud as you walk, move or dance the journey of the text.

Speaking with an Audio Sample

Many people report that their own accent shifts depending on who they are speaking to. It may feel as if another person's accent acts as a magnetic pull on your own. You can recreate this in accent practice by using your audio sample and some headphones.

Put on your headphones, leaving one ear free to hear yourself speak. Turn the volume down low, as if you are in a café sitting next to this American speaker. Begin to speak your text aloud, allowing your voice to be pulled towards the native speaker's sound. You can begin quietly, even just whispering. Slowly increase the volume as you feel comfortable. I encourage you to move around as you speak to root the exercise in your body and breath.

Falling into a Pattern

When transitioning to text, it can start to feel as though you are falling into the same musical pattern on each line. Although there are patterns in any accent, you want to avoid sounding repetitive. I suggest varying your catchphrases so that each phrase sounds a bit different than the other. This will give you three different melodic patterns on which to hook your ear and will lead to variety when speaking the text. Also take care to identify your operative words, as the operative words act as a guide and help you avoid falling into a repetitive melodic pattern.

Asking Questions in a General American Accent

Question phrases in accents other than your own can require a little practice to master. Listen to the questions spoken below in an American accent.

Where's the restroom?

How are you?

Why did you leave?

The way you speak a question will vary depending on the given circumstances. But using simple questions as part of your catchphrase practice will help locate you. Assign a descriptive word to the music of the question. For example, American questions often feel like a press towards the end of the phrase. Draw the journey of the question to visualise if you are you sliding up or down.

Resonance

Resonance refers to the vocal tone and quality of the voice. Every accent has its own distinct way of amplifying the sound. Resonance is what makes some accents sound swallowed while others sound nasal. Resonance is directly influenced by the shape and setting of the mouth, including the lips, tongue, soft palate and throat.

The General American accent is often confused for being overly nasal. In fact, the technical term for the buzz heard in native speakers' voices is *twang*. Twang was identified by American singing coach and voice researcher Jo Estill as a slight squeeze in the tissue folds by the larynx.

An easy and safe way to create twang is speaking or singing with the tongue sitting high in the mouth. Indeed, twang is often heard in accents with a high tongue position like the American accent. You can go back to the High Tongue Position exercise in Chapter 1 in order to troubleshoot this area.

An overly nasal sound stems from the soft palate resting low, allowing for sound to travel up through the nose. Return to the soft-palate exercises in Chapter 1 to encourage a shift.

Working with Resonance

The American accent is sometimes described as buzzy or twangy. While we often restrict our speaking voice to the chest and throat, the American accent can take advantage of resonators in the head, face, soft palate and nose. It may feel as if the sound in the General American accent is bouncing out of all areas of the head and out to the listener.

To achieve this sensation, try the following exercise.

1. Drop the head forward so that your nose is pointing towards the floor.
2. Gently hum into the front of the face, allowing gravity to pull the vibration forward.
3. Keeping the head forward, start to count in the accent whilst aiming the vibration forward on the face: One, two, three, four, five...

4. Gravity will continue to help pull vibration forward as you shift to speaking your text aloud, sensing vibration on the mask of the face.
5. Finally, lift your head, but keep the buzzy sensation in the same area as you continue to speak in accent.

Expanding on this exercise, take time to wake up the resonators and play with them. Have a sense of vibration in each area as you explore. As you do the following exercise, keep your breathing free and allow the throat to stay open.

▶ 10.10

1. Hum into the crown of your head, keeping your breath and throat open throughout. Sense the vibration in the forehead and top of your head. It may be easiest to access by using a pitch slightly higher than your spoken voice.
2. Hum into the nose, sensing a nasal vibration. It may help to think of sounding like a cartoon character.
3. Shake your head back and forth while voicing on a 'Heee'. Allow the sound to fall as if it's coming out of the side of your head.
4. Bounce sound off the roof of your mouth while saying 'Yeah, yeah, yeah, yeah, yeah'. Sense the vibration on the roof of the mouth.
5. Focus a hum to vibrate off the front of your face. It will feel as if there is vibration on your lips and your cheekbones. You can even sense vibration off another surface such as a wall if you stand very close to it when humming.
6. Keeping your throat open, allow the sound to move and centre itself in the throat. Begin to hum in a manner as if you are speaking at a cocktail party. Let this sound be gentle with your throat open.

7. Finally, move the hum into your chest. It may be useful to give the chest some light taps while voicing to feel the vibration bounce.

After warming up the resonators, you can begin to apply the American accent to each area. Start back at the beginning, working your way through them again using the following exercises.

1. In the American accent, count from one to ten using each resonator.
2. Start voicing short phrases in the accent using each resonator. 'Hi, how are you?', 'I'm fine thanks!'
3. Speak a nursery rhyme in the American accent using each resonator.

4. Explore your performance text using each resonator in the accent. See which resonator seems to fit best not only with the accent, but also with your character.

Resonance and Text

Once you find the resonator that fits best with the accent and your character, you can begin to alternate between a resonance prompt – such as the ones in the list below – and your character's text.

1. Direct vibration to the resonator you are using with a simple phrase or prompt. The prompt acts as a quick way to locate and direct vocal vibration in your body.
2. Then allow yourself to weave between your resonance prompt and the text, sensing the vibration in the same area of the body as you switch between the two.

Kendra from Gloria by Branden Jacobs-Jenkins

[Resonance Prompt] One, two, three, four, five...

[Text] A very bad thing happened to both of us! – to all of us!

Yeah, yeah, yeah...

yet you seem to think it happened only to you.

[Hum in the resonator area.]

Why is that?

One, two, three, four, five...

Because you went to Gloria's dumb party and she saved you?

Yeah, yeah, yeah...

Because you were 'a witness' to everyone's last moments?

[*Hum in the resonator area.*]

Helpful Hint: You may want to run through this multiple times. Each time you can slowly reduce the number of times you speak your resonance prompt until you are only speaking the text.

Resonance and Vowels

I encourage you to take time and space in the vowels in order to capture the American accent's resonance. It can be useful to imagine the energy of the accent moving through the vowel sounds as you speak your performance text. Allow yourself to sense the vibration created by speaking in the accent.

Finally...

The music of an accent can take time to master, but there's so much pay-off when it finally clicks. Allow yourself to enjoy and play through the process, just as you would in learning a piece of music. A sense of play will empower you to make your own choices that serve to enhance your text and character.

4. The Performance

There comes a point in all accent work when the actor must move beyond the technical aspects and accent 'rules' in order to bridge the accent into performance. Accent acquisition often begins by focusing on the micro-details. You start by learning the various pronunciations and focus on what's happening in the mouth. However, you don't want the accent to get stuck at the level of the mouth, or the accent may start to sound cosmetic or inauthentic.

Instead, it's important for the accent to become rooted in the body, breath and voice so that the accent feels truly inhabited in performance. The accent also needs to connect with the text and the overall characterisation, including the given circumstances and objectives. This is why good performance requires you to incorporate the accent into the elements of acting.

In order for the accent to feel second nature, you cannot simply play the accent. Although accuracy is important, emotional truth is even more so. This is why you must integrate the accent with your character's intentions and relationships. Ultimately the accent needs to meet the intent of the writer's words to bring the story to life.

Voice vs Accent

Keep in mind that there's a difference between voice and accent. Although they are linked, the voice is key to your interpretation of the character. An accent is merely one facet of the whole of your voice.

All of the following speakers have a 'General' American accent, but sound slightly different from one another. This is because their voice is affected by their age, gender, background and lived experience. So while the voice may change, the accent is similar.

▶ 1.1: *The Wonderful Wizard of Oz*

Warming Up

I have a secret for you: all of the best actors warm up. The warm-up may look a little different from actor to actor, but a skilful actor has a routine that centres them to allow for success in performance. I encourage you to warm up your voice and body with the accent before performing.

Indeed, there is nothing worse than hearing an actor warm up the accent in the first scene. The audience may even become nervous for the actor and question if they should believe the acting or not.

Take the time to properly warm up your body, breath and voice so that the accent can sit comfortably in performance. Get the muscles of speech primed in the accent and ready to go. A simple warm-up will give you freedom and flexibility both on stage and in front of the camera. You can find a sample accent warm-up at the back of this book.

Connecting Accent to the Body

A tight body will lead to an inflexible voice, and an inflexible voice can limit the accent. After you've spent time warming up the whole of the body, use the following exercises to root the accent in your body for an embodied sound.

Merging Voice with Movement

1. Begin by moving around the room in the way that your character moves. Take note of any patterns that arise, including changes of pace, weight or direction.
2. Then start to vocalise. Your voice may be quiet at first and could begin with just sounds, no words. Link your voice with your movement and body so that your voice is a reflection of your character's movements and responding to the body.
3. Then transition to speaking words in the accent as you move. This may include lines from your text or speaking freely in an improvised manner. Sense the merging of movement with the voice.
4. Eventually bring the volume up so you are vocalising at the same volume you might speak to someone standing in the same room. Continue to move and speak, allowing your body and voice to integrate and influence each other.

Some actors like to find the voice of their character first and then discover the way that character moves. Other actors prefer discovering the character's movement and rooting themselves in the body before finding the voice. There is no right answer here – both the voice and the body of the character will influence each other. Linking these two pieces together brings your voice and accent to a more fully embodied place.

Sun Salutation

Sun salutations tend to be the perfect exercise when an actor feels 'stuck' in the accent, and the accent feels unembodied.

1. Take a deep breath in as you reach your arms up over your head.
2. Swan dive down while speaking lines aloud from your text, or free speaking in the accent.
3. Lift up halfway before releasing your torso to hang over your legs again.
4. Kick back into a plank, continuing to speak aloud in the accent.
5. Come down flat to the ground and gently lift your upper back halfway up to a low cobra or fully up to an upward-facing dog.
6. Press back into a downward-facing dog and peddle out the feet as you continue to speak aloud.
7. Walk, step or jump your feet to your hands.
8. Lift up halfway before releasing your torso again to hang over your legs.
9. Continue speaking as you roll your way back up into standing.
10. Finish by releasing your arms down to your sides.

You can take a breath in at any point in this sequence, although it's usually best to breathe in when the body lifts, such as in cobra or upward-facing dog. Repeat this sequence a number of times, maybe three or even five times through. After you've completed the sequence, speak your text aloud without the sun salutation, and allow yourself to feel any changes in your body, voice or accent.

Accent and Chakras

One way to recentre the accent in your voice and body is to employ the imaginative use of chakras.

In the East, chakras are thought to be centres of consciousness. In the West, chakras are sometimes considered centres of energetic fields, roughly corresponding to glands in the endocrine system. These backgrounds have inspired actors to use chakras as imaginative tools to enhance their understanding of character and emotion. Some practitioners using chakras in their work include American actor trainer Fay Simpson in her book *The Lucid Body* and American dialect coach Beth McGuire in her book *How to Do African Accents*.

For our purposes, the use of chakras is as an imaginative tool for the performer. Each chakra corresponds to a central point in the body and is thought to be associated with human behaviour. This can be useful to an actor when playing with character, circumstance and objectives. However, you do not need to 'believe' in chakras to complete the exercise. In fact, many actors find new discoveries about their character and the accent after exploring the chakras.

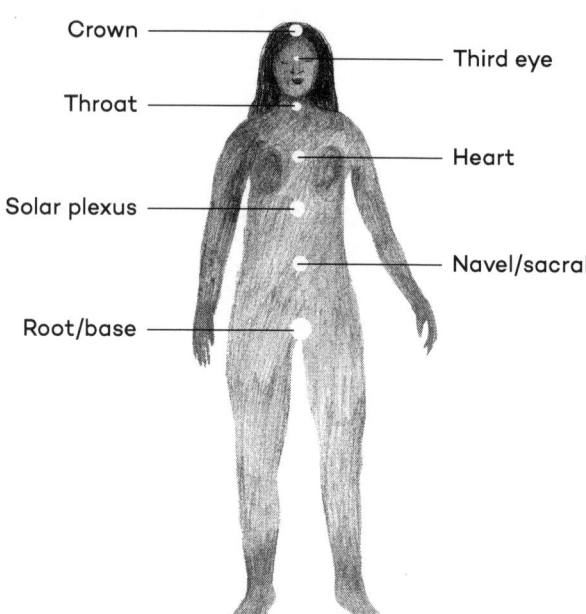

- The *root or base chakra* is located in the low hips and groin. It represents the body, grounding, stability, security, courage – and also survival, violence, greed and anger.
- The *navel or sacral chakra* is located at the belly button and around the sacral space just below. It represents emotions, sensuality, sexuality, desire, pleasure – and also shame and jealousy.
- The *solar plexus chakra* is located below the ribcage. It represents will, personal power, authority, laughter, energy – and also fear and hate.
- The *heart chakra* is found in the chest. It represents love, understanding, balance, peace – and also a blocked heart or cold-heartedness.
- The *throat chakra* is located on the front of the throat. It represents communication and expression through the spoken word.

- The *third eye* is located on the spot between the eyebrows. It represents thinking, wisdom, intuition, intelligence and imagination.
- The *crown chakra* is located on the top of the head. It represents belief, truth and the higher self.

According to American actor trainer Fay Simpson, 'the three lower centres, closest to the ground, constitute the survival energies… while the three higher centers relate to the more intuitive, mental, and abstract energies.' The heart chakra acts as a bridge between the higher and lower chakras.

Exploring Voice and Accent Through the Chakras

Take some time to explore moving the accent through each chakra. You can do the following exploration lying on your back, standing or moving:

1. Imagine or visualise that your voice is living deep in your hips in the root chakra.
2. Allow yourself some time to direct your awareness into this area.
3. You may want to place your hands on or around this area of your body. Take a moment to direct your breath to this area of your body.
4. Then start a gentle hum as if the sound is originating from this chakra. The hum may feel quite deep and low, but you can play around with a pitch that feels right.
5. Finally, speak a line of text in the accent as if your voice is connected to this chakra.

Continue this exercise through each successive chakra, moving up through the body:

1. Bring your attention up to your navel chakra by your belly button. Visualise that your breath and a hum are originating from this area of your body. Repeat your line of text while keeping your connection to this area.
2. Then repeat this sequence at the solar plexus, below your ribcage.
3. Move the accent and voice up again, speaking this time as if the line of text is coming from your heart chakra in your chest.
4. Continue up to the throat chakra, taking care to allow this area to stay open and released while you hum and then speak a line of text.
5. Bring the exercise up into the third eye area between your eyebrows.
6. Finally, speak your line of text as if it's coming from the crown chakra. The voice at this point may sound much different than it did when you began down at the root chakra.

Choosing a Chakra for Performance

Now that you've explored all of the chakras, see if there is one chakra that resonates with your character. Based on the descriptions of each chakra, choose one to which your character may have a connection.

1. Bring your attention to the chosen chakra and allow yourself to focus on this area of the body, placing your attention there.
2. Start a gentle hum and imagine your voice originating from this area of the body.
3. Then begin speaking your text aloud from this chakra, as if your voice is residing in this area of your body.
4. After speaking your text aloud, notice any changes or new connections you've found in the accent.

After exploring one chakra in detail, you may want to explore a few more chakras in-depth for your character. Sense how changing the chakra changes your connection with the body, voice and even the overall delivery.

You may choose to layer or move between two or even three chakras in performance. However, simply touching base with one chakra can help to ground the accent back into the voice and body of your character.

Playing with Range

Sometimes you may feel that the accent is 'locked' or feels very one-note. This may be because the accent isn't free enough in your voice to allow for a range of vocal choices.

Exploring different dynamics within your voice in the accent can help free the accent up. These dynamics may include pace, pitch and range while speaking in the accent. An accent sitting comfortably within the dynamics of the voice should allow you to use the whole of your voice in the accent.

It's important to give yourself permission to play with your voice in the accent. Playfulness not only makes the process fun, but it also frees up any unnecessary tension.

Roller-coaster Voice

This is an exercise that I've called Roller-coaster Voice because it sounds as if your voice is riding a roller-coaster. Additionally, an actor I worked with once said this exercise reminded him of Dory from *Finding Nemo* 'speaking whale', and is similar to the Pulling Faces exercise.

1. Begin by warming up your voice with some gentle vocal sirens using a lip trill. Explore the highs and lows of your voice as you gently open up your pitch range.
2. Then transition to speaking your text aloud in the accent.
3. Start opening up the pitch range as you move from the highs and lows of your voice. This is when it may feel as if your voice is going on a roller-coaster ride.
4. Allow yourself as much as possible to explore the extremes, reaching both the high highs and low lows of your voice.
5. Finally, speak your text aloud from the beginning as normal. Your voice may find itself newly centred. Often the accent feels more grounded after this exercise.

Alternating Voices

You may feel as if your voice tends to switch registers, jumping up or down in pitch when speaking in a new accent. This sensation is often reported by actors and there is a concern that the accent doesn't 'feel real'. If you want the accent to be pitched similarly to your own voice, it can be useful to return to own your voice as a guide.

1. Begin by speaking a sentence of your text in your own voice. Take note of where you sense your voice in your body and pitch range.
2. Then repeat the same sentence in an American accent. Try to match the pitch you felt speaking in your own voice, even in this different accent.
3. Continue this exercise, alternating between speaking aloud in your voice and speaking aloud in the accent. Use your own voice as the anchor.

4. Finally, speak the entire text in the accent. Sense any changes that have occurred. Your voice in the accent should now feel closer to your own voice.

Not every character will need to sound like you, but it is essential to feel that the accent is coming from you. This is also an excellent exercise to explore the character's intentions, both in your voice and in the accent. The exercise gives you a centre in the accent from which to explore.

Exploring Vocal Range in an Accent

You will want to explore a range of scenarios in the accent to feel fully free to play. This exploration allows you to adapt to any situation. Once you feel comfortable using the accent in many situations, there is no limit to how you can use it.

You can do the following explorations using a piece of text or speaking freely.

Speak in the accent aloud as if...

- speaking to a crowd of two hundred people
- speaking to a child
- speaking to a partner in bed
- speaking in a business meeting
- talking on the phone
- telling someone off
- in a nightclub

Create your own additional scenarios which mimic scenarios your character might find themselves in.

You can also rehearse for a range of performance circumstances where you might need to use the accent.

This will allow you to adjust the accent for the performance space.

Speak in the accent aloud as if...

- onstage at Shakespeare's Globe
- onstage in a small black-box theatre
- on camera in a close-up shot
- on camera in a wide shot
- speaking into a microphone
- outside in a large square performing for a crowd of passing onlookers

An accent needs to adjust to the space it's being performed in, just like you adjust your acting to fit the size and scale of your performance. A large space might call for a larger voice and, by extension, a larger accent. The accent may feel slightly different between spaces – that is entirely normal.

Connecting Accent to Text

As an actor, your most vital job is to tell the story. It's all well and good to be able to do an accent, but in performance the accent should not overshadow the words on the page. The text is your road map, and an accent needs to integrate seamlessly in order to bring the story to life.

I encourage you to root the accent in the text through practising classic voice and text exercises in the accent. The following exercises help bridge the accent from technical drills to full artistry in performance.

One Word at a Time

The goal of this exercise is to reconnect your breath to the words on the page and to the length of thought.

Practise this exercise first by using only numbers.

1. Start by counting aloud the number 'one' in an American accent.
2. Then add the next number each subsequent round: One, two...
3. Continue to add a number as you progress: One, two, three... / One, two, three, four... / One, two, three, four, five...

Notice your breath at the beginning of each round. The key here is to be in touch with your breathing, and to match your breath to the length of thought. As you go up in numbers, the breath capacity will need to increase.

Then transition to using your text.

1. Begin by speaking the first word aloud: 'I...'
2. Then add the next word of the phrase on each subsequent round: 'I am...'
3. Continue to add a word each round, slowly building the thought as you go:
   a) 'I am going...'
   b) 'I am going to...'
   c) 'I am going to the...'
   d) 'I am going to the store.'

You may want to break this process up by sentences or in sections.

Just as before, notice your breathing and allow your breath to match the length of the thought. Be sure to connect with each word as well. Really hear the word as it leaves your mouth and is spoken aloud. It can be useful to have a sense that you are aiming each phrase towards a specific point in the room.

This exercise is vital as it allows you to reconnect the accent to your breathing and to the words in the text.

Mouth the Words

Another way to connect to the text is to turn the voice off completely and simply to mouth the words in the accent. Begin by mouthing the text in the accent silently, without even a whisper.

Allow yourself to feel the choreography that your mouth goes through when speaking the text in the accent. Take care to stay connected to your breathing as you complete this exercise. Nervous actors have a tendency to switch into shallow breathing, which can be a tell that the accent is not 'real'. Use your breath to connect with and support your thoughts, even when your voice is silent.

Then go back to the beginning and read the text again, this time aloud. Make a note of any changes that you pick up. You may feel that your breath is more connected. The muscles of the mouth may relax as well. At this stage the muscles are now awake and can release while maintaining precision in the accent.

Making the Text and Accent Physical

A good writer writes with the character's voice in mind: all of their rhythms, pacing and dynamics are written into the lines, waiting for you to discover them. You will begin to notice these by making the text physical. The following exercises are wonderful for getting you out of your head and into your body. The voice and accent will follow as the accent's rhythms become fused with the text in performance.

1. Walk while speaking the text aloud in the accent. Switch directions after every full stop.
2. Walk while speaking the text aloud in the accent. Change directions after each punctuation mark (full stop, comma, semi-colon, dash, etc.).
3. Walk while speaking the text aloud in the accent. Gently tap an object in the room on the last word of each sentence. Be sure to make contact with the object at the same time you speak the last word in the sentence aloud.
4. Physicalise the text in the accent. Bring the text and accent to life by creating shapes with your body while speaking aloud. This exercise may feel a bit like an interpretive dance. Allow your body to express the words, images and thoughts on the page. Equally, allow your voice to match your movement.

Go back to the top and speak the text aloud from the beginning as normal after each of these exercises. Make note of anything new you've discovered in the text and accent.

All of the above exercises rely on what British voice coach Barbara Houseman terms 'layering'. As described earlier, layering means you focus on one element at a time in the exercise. After the exercise, you then let go of the element you just explored, trusting that your body will retain the experience and the muscle memory of what you've learnt. You then move on to adding another layer and repeating the process. Take the exercises one at a time, and trust that the body will access what it needs through the technique.

Connecting Accent to Character

The way people speak reveals a lot about them – where they are from, their lived experience, and even who they aspire to be. This means that an accent is more than the sum of its parts. Speech patterns can become an audible representation of the entire character. I like to imagine if there is a person in the world who could be this character and then try to find that voice somewhere online or in real life. However, keep in mind that it is not necessary to find – and mimic – an actor who has played the role you are playing before. Instead you are looking for someone in real life who might inspire the creation of this character.

The way a person speaks can reveal the human behind an accent. Take time to connect the accent back to the character. The voice and accent should be specific to the character you are playing for each role.

Using Catchphrases

One actor I worked with was playing a cut-throat executive at the top of her field. The actor and I decided together that her character needed to sound sharp and smooth. This was a character who knew what to say and how to say it. I found a clip of an American saying 'You gotta do what you gotta do' in a very cool manner. It felt as if the words were smooth and cold as ice as they left her mouth. We went through the text and applied this as a catchphrase so that the words took on a sleek quality. The actor would use that line from time to time to reground herself in the accent but also to access the voice of the character. In this sense, the short catchphrase allowed the actor to transform into her character for performance.

Vocal Quality

Another actor I worked with had a role in a horror film playing the bad guy. He wanted his character's voice to be raspy and deep with an eerie quality to it. We worked together to explore different areas of the character's voice in the accent. We decided that the voice and accent should 'live' in the chest. This provided a physical grounding for the actor. Centring the accent in the body became a way that he could connect with the overall accent without thinking of the technical 'rules'. We also worked to safely add raspiness so that the actor could create the sound without losing his voice. By connecting with his voice and body, the actor gained an access point to the accent. The end result was ear-catching and fit the character perfectly.

Status

I worked with two actors playing opposite each other, where one character was in control and the other character was being controlled. Both actors were speaking in the same accent, but it was clear these were two radically different characters. The character with the lower status found a voice and accent that was very staccato and a little skittish. Her voice was high-pitched and almost floating across the room. The dominant character accessed a voice that was weighty, powerful and domineering.

This is an example of how the accent must adapt depending on the character. In this case, status affects the characters and their vocal quality completely. Status might change the rhythm and pacing of the accent, even if both characters are using the same accent.

Additionally, these two actors playing opposite each other really had to listen to each other and respond to their partners accordingly. Each night the performance and accent characterisations were a bit different as the actors adjusted based on their scene partner.

Finally…

The most valuable aspect you bring to the table is your own personal point of view. Thousands of actors have played Hamlet, but the 'best' Hamlet is up to interpretation. That's because each Hamlet is unique – and based on the actor's choices.

Accent work is just one aspect that goes into building a character. It is simply a layer of storytelling. You are allowed to make choices regarding the accent beyond the technical rules. In fact, I strongly encourage you to play and have fun with the accent, particularly as you move into making the accent your own. This will not only make the process more enjoyable and rewarding, but it will also render the accent more alive, more embodied, and more authentic in performance.

5. Accent Warm-up

Initial Stretches

- Begin by stretching out your upper body. Loosen your neck and shoulders.
- Then flop over from the waist and breathe into your lower back and belly. Slowly come back up to standing.

Connecting Movement to the Breath

- Circle your hips around while releasing your voice on a long, slow S. Reverse the direction of the circling and release your voice on a long, slow Z.
- Circle your ribcage around while releasing your voice on a long, slow S. Reverse the direction of the circling and release your voice on a long, slow Z.
- Roll your shoulders backwards while releasing your voice on a long slow S. Reverse the direction of the circling and release your voice on a long, slow Z.
- Drop your head and neck and gently circle while releasing your voice on a long, slow S. Reverse the direction of the circling and release your voice on a long, slow Z.

Lip and Tongue Trills

- Gently expand your vocal range whilst blowing air through your lips like horse lips. Equally, you can roll your tongue if that is easier. Bring vibration and sound to this action. Allow your voice to go from high to low and then from low to high.

Lip and Voice Stretches

- Allow your voice to siren down from high to low, switching back and forth from 'OO-EE-OO-EE-OO'. Really allow your lips flexibility as they move between rounding and spreading to make these vowels.

Pulling Faces

- Start by softly chewing, followed by raising the eyebrows and scrunching the cheeks. Finish by moving your entire face around, as if moving the air in front of your face.
- Make some gentle sounds with your voice as you are moving your face.

Face Massage

- Begin with the temples and then massage your jaw, sinuses, forehead and chin.
- You can also focus a gentle massage on the facial pressure points:
    1. The temples on either side of your head.
    2. The masseter muscle in your jaw sitting in front of your ears.

3. On either side of your nose by the nostrils.
4. On your brow bone where it meets the top of your nose and eye sockets.

Yawn with the Lips Closed

- Provoke a yawn and feel a parachute-like stretch in the soft palate in the back of your mouth.

Tongue Stretch

- Rest the tip of your tongue behind your bottom teeth. Allow the middle of the tongue to cascade forward out of the front of your mouth. Sense a stretch in the tongue root.

Tongue Circles

- Place your tongue between your lips and teeth. Circle the tongue around the teeth five times to each side with your lips closed. It may feel as if you are cleaning your teeth with your tongue. Swallow at the end to release any tension.

Tongue Reset

- Rest your tongue flat on your bottom lip outside of your mouth. Feel the middle back of the tongue engaging to form the consonants L and R. Keep the tip of your tongue resting down.

  Eleven yellow lemons rolled rapidly down the road.

Resonance

- Hum into the crown of your head, keeping your breath and throat open throughout. Sense the vibration in your forehead and top of your head. It may be easiest to access using a pitch slightly higher than your spoken voice.
- Hum into the nose, sensing a nasal vibration. It may help to think of it sounding like a cartoon character.
- Shake your head back and forth while voicing 'EE'. Allow the sound to fall as if it's coming out of the side of your head.
- Bounce sound off the roof of your mouth while saying 'Yeah, yeah, yeah, yeah, yeah'. Sense the vibration on the roof of your mouth.
- Focus a hum to vibrate off the front of your face. It may feel as if there is vibration on your lips and cheekbones.
- Keeping your throat open, allow the sound to move and centre itself in the throat. Begin to hum and babble as if you are speaking at a cocktail party.
- Finally, move the hum into your chest. It may be useful to give your chest and upper back some light taps while voicing to feel the vibration bounce.

Speak your catchphrases or phrases from the text from each of these resonance areas.

Counting in the Accent

- Take three rounds of counting aloud in the accent as long as you can without straining. Reconnect with your breathing on each round.

Swear Words in the Accent

- A string of swear words in the accent is a simple way to access the mouth of the accent and to wake your speech muscles up as you fully commit to the words.

Practice Sentences in the Accent

- Speak some practice sentences or tongue-twisters aloud to activate the accent in your mouth.

Catchphrases

- Alternate your catchphrases with some text.

Text Check-in

- Speak any tricky words or difficult passage of text aloud in advance to get the muscles primed in your mouth before performance.
- Mouth bits of text silently to feel the muscles of your mouth engaged. Connect with your breathing to allow your breath to power the voice and accent.

Full List of Practice Sentences

All these practice sentences can be heard online at:
bit.ly/mastering-an-american-accent-audio-recordings

Accessing the American Tongue

Eleven yellow lemons rolled rapidly down the road.

Rachel had a hard start to the race, but she got better over time and won the prize fair and square.

Recently police learned that Larry stole millions of dollars from the hospital.

R Sentences

The customer is at the centre of a major internal error.

We searched over the entire Earth to find the person responsible for the work.

The colonel murdered the girl for her pearls.

Some teenagers were forever gathering early at the church on the other side of Denver.

The two sisters wrote many letters over the years to their brothers.

Anders owns four pairs of runner's trousers.

The kindergartners read two chapters of the school director's book.

America is famous for its pizza and hamburgers.

The idea of being in Florida in August sounds terrible to Lydia and me.

Let me tell you the saga about Donna and me after drinking too much vodka on the rocks.

OR as in FORCE

We will use torture or force only as a last resort.

The warrior stood before his wardrobe door in order to find her sword.

It's horribly adorable to give horoscope advice to a Californian orange.

AR as in START

As far as I'm concerned, the partying has gone too far.

He's barking mad if he thinks he can park the car near the farmer's yard.

She's an absolute martyr for darning the socks with yarn.

AIR as in SQUARE

Mary got married and she was very merry.

The bear put some pear in his hair and called it self-care.

We won the dare, fair and square.

EER as in NEAR

Be of good cheer, dear!

The cashier was sincere when ringing up the price of beer.

Seriously, the experience was a spiritual miracle.

L Sentences

L at the Beginning of a Word

Liam looks a lot like his sister Lucy.

Let's look at that problem later.

Lydia leaned in and laughed loudly.

L Before a Vowel

They freely follow the leader of the cult.

I put eleven dollars in my wallet before I left the house.

My family doesn't like olives, but we love melon.

L at the End of a Word

Are you available to call her at twelve o'clock?

A successful judicial clerk is practical and professional.

The terrible football team lost because they were too physical on the field.

T Sentences

The Flap T

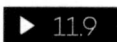

The firefighter's daughter is a writer.

We water the tomatoes on Saturday.

There are little butterflies all over the city.

I'm pretty sure that Peter has the water bottle.

It doesn't matter if the rider is getting thirsty.

Consonant T Pronounced

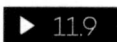

The hotel has seventeen rooms.

Do all guitar players have tattoos?

He's pretending to protect himself from attack.

The Canadian dentist's dog likes to go on walks in the daytime.

T at the End of a Word

I hate being apart from my friend.

I don't have much faith in what's going on out there.

I don't want that.

A lot of weight is put on the table.

Get out of the way before you get in the car.

Sit at the foot of the bed.

Letter T Near the Letter N

The button on the mitten is hidden.

Martin is writing sentences about mountains.

I'm giving you an important letter to deliver to Mr Barton.

The Word 'To'

What do I need to do for you tomorrow?

I'm going to the store.

All I want you to do is to love me.

Vowels

/æ/ as in TRAP

▶ 11.13

Mac will be in the shadows holding a hat at the top of Act Two.

Half of all cats have their vaccinations against rat bacteria.

The fact is that sapphire does not flatter me at all.

Staff have a hard time controlling the questions asked by the class.

I would rather take a bath than complete a task.

AN, AM and ANG

▶ 11.14

Nancy can't stand transporting plants in the trunk of her car.

Dan and I had the chance to dance the night away at my aunt's party.

The archaeologist took a sample from the land next to the Amazon.

/ɑ/ as in SPA, LOT and THOUGHT

▶ 11.15

Tom is talking to Paul about his daughter's law school.

I bought a cup of coffee while walking my dog.

The restaurant boss didn't like that the water came at no cost to the throngs of customers.

The jolly toddler knocked over the tower of blocks and balls.

It's best to be honest about the knowledge you have and not get caught in a naughty lie!

/ɑ/ as in SPA vs OR /ɔɚ/ as in FORCE

The court of law in North Australia awarded John four hundred dollars.

We all saw that our father was sore after his fall in Cornwall.

George bought a new door to transform the awful cottage into an adorable home.

/oʊ/ as in GOAT

▶ 11.17

Row row row your boat…

Soak the noble's robe in soap and rose water.

Joan's family is nobility from Rome, and she isn't below acting holier than we know her to be.

She wrapped her toes in ropes before floating out in the ocean in a boat.

/oʊ/ as in GOAL

The old man told me he has a cold.

Don't forget to go slowly when you fold the clothes.

Paul says to call Cole before buying that pole at the mall.

Stress and Pronunciation

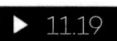

The princess is frustrated about the controversy surrounding her love to donate.

After Thanksgiving, the adult recluse went to the ballet and got a massage.

Rosemary's territory is near the military's supply of strawberries.

The Kit List

Keyword	GenAm Phonetics	Example Words from GenAm
FLEECE	iː	eat, sees, Caesar, be
KIT	ɪ	big, pretty, myth, biscuit
DRESS	ɛ	pet, bread, ready, friend
TRAP	æ	cat, plaid, dapper, dad
BATH	æ	glass, rather, path, half
PALM	ɑː	father, calm, spa, lager
LOT	ɑ	stop, honest, knowledge
CLOTH	ɑ ~ ɔ	cough, often, off, across
THOUGHT	ɑ ~ ɔ	bought, August, autumn, jaw
GOOSE	uː	food, shoes, mood, you
FOOT	ʊ	good, cushion, cook, should
STRUT	ʌ̈	love, done, touch, blood
FACE	eɪ	stage, April, wait, change
PRICE	aɪ	high, Friday, right, tribe

Keyword	GenAm Phonetics	Example Words from GenAm
CHOICE	ɔɪ	boy, employ, poison, joy
GOAT	oʊ	home, soap, noble, old
MOUTH	aʊ	sound, count, now, around
NURSE	ɚ ~ ɝ	turn, heard, word, verb
NORTH	ɔɚ	normal, war, for, short
FORCE	ɔɚ	floor, four, deport, explore
START	ɑɚ	car, hard, sharp, party
SQUARE	eɚ	fair, dare, bear, parent
NEAR	ɪɚ	clear, fear, dear, cashier
CURE	ʊɚ ~ ɚ	sure, your, assurance, Europe
COMM<u>A</u>	ə	ide<u>a</u>, Emm<u>a</u>, pizz<u>a</u>, <u>a</u>bout
LETT<u>ER</u>	ɚ	act<u>or</u>, sug<u>ar</u>, bigg<u>er</u>, fail<u>ure</u>

International Phonetic Alphabet Chart

CONSONANTS (PULMONIC)

	Bilabial	Labiodental	Dental	Alveolar	Postalveolar	Retroflex	Palatal	Velar	Uvular	Pharyngeal	Glottal
Plosive	p b			t d		ʈ ɖ	c ɟ	k ɡ	q ɢ		ʔ
Nasal	m	ɱ		n		ɳ	ɲ	ŋ	ɴ		
Trill	ʙ			r					ʀ		
Tap or Flap		ⱱ		ɾ		ɽ					
Fricative	ɸ β	f v	θ ð	s z	ʃ ʒ	ʂ ʐ	ç ʝ	x ɣ	χ ʁ	ħ ʕ	h ɦ
Lateral fricative				ɬ ɮ							
Approximant		ʋ		ɹ		ɻ	j	ɰ			
Lateral approximant				l		ɭ	ʎ	ʟ			

Symbols to the right in a cell are voiced, to the left are voiceless. Shaded areas denote articulations judged impossible.

CONSONANTS (NON-PULMONIC)

Clicks	Voiced implosives	Ejectives
ʘ Bilabial	ɓ Bilabial	ʼ Examples:
ǀ Dental	ɗ Dental/alveolar	pʼ Bilabial
ǃ (Postalveolar)	ʄ Palatal	tʼ Dental/alveolar
ǂ Palatoalveolar	ɠ Velar	kʼ Velar
ǁ Alveolar lateral	ʛ Uvular	sʼ Alveolar fricative

VOWELS

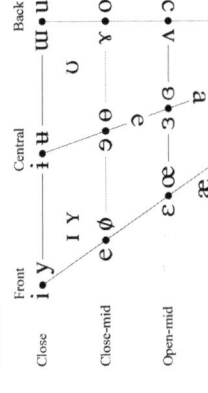

Where symbols appear in pairs, the one to the right represents a rounded vowel.

© 2015 IPA

OTHER SYMBOLS

ʍ Voiceless labial-velar fricative	ɕ ʑ Alveolo-palatal fricatives
w Voiced labial-velar approximant	ɺ Voiced alveolar lateral flap
ɥ Voiced labial-palatal approximant	ɧ Simultaneous ʃ and x
ʜ Voiceless epiglottal fricative	
ʢ Voiced epiglottal fricative	Affricates and double articulations can be represented by two symbols joined by a tie bar if necessary. t͡s k͡p
ʡ Epiglottal plosive	

DIACRITICS Some diacritics may be placed above a symbol with a descender, e.g. ŋ̊

̥	Voiceless	n̥ d̥	̤	Breathy voiced	b̤ a̤	̪	Dental	t̪ d̪
̬	Voiced	s̬ t̬	̰	Creaky voiced	b̰ a̰	̺	Apical	t̺ d̺
ʰ	Aspirated	tʰ dʰ	̼	Linguolabial	t̼ d̼	̻	Laminal	t̻ d̻
̹	More rounded	ɔ̹	ʷ	Labialized	tʷ dʷ	̃	Nasalized	ẽ
̜	Less rounded	ɔ̜	ʲ	Palatalized	tʲ dʲ	ⁿ	Nasal release	dⁿ
̟	Advanced	u̟	ˠ	Velarized	tˠ dˠ	ˡ	Lateral release	dˡ
̠	Retracted	e̠	ˤ	Pharyngealized	tˤ dˤ	̚	No audible release	d̚
̈	Centralized	ë	̴	Velarized or pharyngealized	ɫ			
̽	Mid-centralized	ẽ	̝	Raised	e̝ (ɹ̝ = voiced alveolar fricative)			
̩	Syllabic	n̩	̞	Lowered	e̞ (β̞ = voiced bilabial approximant)			
̯	Non-syllabic	e̯	̘	Advanced Tongue Root	e̘			
˞	Rhoticity	ɚ a˞	̙	Retracted Tongue Root	e̙			

SUPRASEGMENTALS

ˈ	Primary stress	ˌfoʊnəˈtɪʃən
ˌ	Secondary stress	
ː	Long	eː
ˑ	Half-long	eˑ
̆	Extra-short	ĕ
|	Minor (foot) group	
‖	Major (intonation) group	
.	Syllable break	ɹi.ækt
‿	Linking (absence of a break)	

TONES AND WORD ACCENTS

LEVEL			CONTOUR		
e̋	or ˥	Extra high	ě	or ˇ	Rising
é	˦	High	ê	ˆ	Falling
ē	˧	Mid	e᷄	᷄	High rising
è	˨	Low	e᷅	᷅	Low rising
ȅ	˩	Extra low	e᷈	᷈	Rising-falling
↓	Downstep		↗	Global rise	
↑	Upstep		↘	Global fall	

http://www.internationalphoneticassociation.org/content/ipa-chart, available under a Creative Commons Attribution-Sharealike 3.0 Unported License. Copyright © 2015 International Phonetic Association

The Wonderful Wizard of Oz by L. Frank Baum (1900)

▶ 1.1

Dorothy lived in the midst of the great Kansas prairies, with Uncle Henry, who was a farmer, and Aunt Em, who was the farmer's wife. Their house was small, for the lumber to build it had to be carried by wagon many miles. There were four walls, a floor and a roof, which made one room; and this room contained a rusty looking cookstove, a cupboard for the dishes, a table, three or four chairs, and the beds. Uncle Henry and Aunt Em had a big bed in one corner, and Dorothy a little bed in another corner. There was no garret at all, and no cellar – except a small hole dug in the ground, called a cyclone cellar, where the family could go in case one of those great whirlwinds arose, mighty enough to crush any building in its path. It was reached by a trap door in the middle of the floor, from which a ladder led down into the small, dark hole.

When Dorothy stood in the doorway and looked around, she could see nothing but the great gray prairie on every side. Not a tree nor a house broke the broad sweep of flat country that reached to the edge of the sky. The sun had baked the plowed land into a gray mass, with little cracks running through it. Even the grass was not green, for the sun had burned the tops of the long blades until they were the same gray color to be seen everywhere. Once the house had been painted, but the sun blistered the paint and the rains washed it away, and now the house was as dull and gray as everything else.

References

L. Frank Baum, *The Wonderful Wizard of Oz*, Chicago/New York City: G.M. Hill Co., 1900.

Cicely Berry, *Voice and the Actor,* New York City: Wiley Publishing, 1973, pp. 66-9.

Barbara Houseman, *Finding Your Voice*, London: Nick Hern Books, 2002, p. 9.

Dudley Knight, *Speaking with Skill*, London: Bloomsbury Methuen Drama, 2012.

Beth McGuire, *African Accents: A Workbook for Actors*, New York City: Routledge, 2016.

Patsy Rodenburg, *The Actors Speaks*, London: Bloomsbury Methuen Drama, 1997.

Fay Simpson, *The Lucid Body*, New York City: Allworth Press, 2008, p. 33

J.C. Wells, *Accents of English*, Cambridge: Cambridge University Press, 1982, p. 120.

Referenced Plays

All these plays are published in the UK by Nick Hern Books, London.

'Prior', *Angels in America: Millennium Approaches* by Tony Kushner, Act Three, Scene Six, p. 118

'Harper', *Angels in America: Perestroika* by Tony Kushner, Act Four, Scene Eight, pp. 284–5

'Zack', *Belleville* by Amy Herzog, Scene One, p. 23

'Kathy', *Clybourne Park* by Bruce Norris, Act Two, p. 71

'Joanne', *Company* by Stephen Sondheim and George Furth, Act One, p. 38

'Jess', *Cost of Living* by Martyna Majok, Scene Three, p. 45

'Avery', *The Flick* by Annie Baker, Act One, Scene Eight, p. 64

'Dean', *Gloria* by Branden Jacobs-Jenkins, Act Two, Scene One, p. 53

'Kendra', *Gloria* by Branden Jacobs-Jenkins, Act Two, Scene One, p. 57

'Erik', *The Humans* by Stephen Karam, p. 29

'Elias', *John* by Annie Baker, Act Two, Scene One, pp. 64–5

'Becca', *Rabbit Hole* by David Lindsay-Abaire, Act One, Scene Four, p. 54

'Diwata', *Speech & Debate* by Stephen Karam, Scene Three, pp. 25–6

'Cynthia', *Sweat* by Lynn Nottage, Act One, Scene Two, p. 29

'Richard', *Teenage Dick* by Mike Lew, Scene One, p. 14

Acknowledgements

A book cannot be written without an immense amount of support behind the author.

Thank you to Matt Applewhite at Nick Hern Books for shepherding this book through its beginning stages all the way until the end.

Thank you to Deirdre McLaughlin for her sage words, her guidance, and for reading the book multiple times through.

Thank you to my many teachers and mentors, including: Linda Gates, Barbara Houseman, William Conacher, Jeannette Nelson, Patsy Rodenburg, Beth McGuire, Fay Simpson, Amy Chaffee, many people at Knight-Thompson Speechwork and many many many more.

Thank you to Marie-Charlotte Brédon Nightingale for her beautiful illustrations and creative spirit.

Thank you to Gurkiran Kaur for her input and guidance on chakras and the voice.

Thank you to the voices that brought this book to life: Ace Anderson, Adriano Cabral, Hanna Gaffney, Eric Jerome Harper, Anne Hollister, Deirdre McLaughlin, Michael Silberblatt, Joel Trill and Will Wilhelm.

Thank you to my colleagues and friends who supported me through the process and offered their valuable thoughts and opinions.

Thank you to my family for their unwavering love.

Finally, thank you to every actor I have had the pleasure of coaching. You have taught me everything I know.

www.nickhernbooks.co.uk

facebook.com/nickhernbooks

twitter.com/nickhernbooks